TEACHING ART
AT KEY STAGE 1

You don't need to be good at art to teach it well

Nigel Meager

Assisted by a grant from CALOUSTE GULBENKIAN FOUNDATION

NSEAD
NATIONAL SOCIETY FOR EDUCATION IN ART & DESIGN

West Cyngor
Glamorgan Sir
County Gorllewin
Council Morgannwg

VISUAL IMPACT PUBLICATIONS

CONTENTS

36   COLOUR

50 FORM

59 SPACE

64 TONE

70 TEXTURE

78 LINE AND MARK

85 APPENDIX

86 INDEX

PREFACE

For the past fifteen years West Glamorgan Education Authority has been supporting projects that place artists in schools. In 1980, the Art Advisor in West Glamorgan, Ceri Barclay, helped to establish an education service at the Glynn Vivian Art Gallery (the gallery is managed by Swansea City Council). This service went on to organise many projects where artists either worked with children in the gallery or in schools. In recent years many other such projects have been organised by artists and educators. The Welsh Arts Council and West Wales Arts (the regional arts association) have been supporting these artist in school and artist in gallery projects in the region.

It was within this context that in 1988 a group of artists and headteachers,who were all very positive about the benefits of artists working in schools, secured support from the Calouste Gulbenkian Foundation, West Glamorgan Education Authority and the Welsh Arts Council. This new project was called Visual Impact.

The aim was to allow artists to work with primary school children in partnership with the class teachers. The idea was that the artists would be classroom based visual advisors.

They would not concentrate on their own work as artists but would offer the wider benefits of their training and professional expertise about art and the visual world in general. Teachers would learn about art from the artists and artists would learn from teachers about what was practical in the classroom. Right from the start it was hoped that new or improved ways of teaching art to young children would develop.

Two artists, Nigel Meager and David Petts, remained close to the project throughout and subsequently have been involved in disseminating the teaching strategies that were developed. This book describes many of those strategies. A crucial test as to whether an idea could be included in this publication was whether the approach could be adopted by a teacher who has no background in art.

Teachers don't need to be good at art to teach it well. The subtext for this is that art, craft and design can be taught using the same kinds of teaching skills that good teachers practice day after day. It became clear that there are many ways in which the qualities needed for good teaching are similar to those needed to create art. There is much in this book that is not in itself new. The artists learnt a great deal about teaching art at Key Stage 1 by observing methods already tried and tested by teachers.

The Visual Impact Project ran for three years from 1989 to 1992. It was based in three schools in West Glamorgan, Craigcefnparc, Craigfelen and Felindre Primary Schools. However ideas from the project have since been tried in a number of different education authorities and many different schools. The Calouste Gulbenkian Foundation and West Glamorgan Education Authority became Visual Impact's major sponsors.

INTRODUCTION

DEVELOPING VISUAL PERCEPTION AND THE VISUAL LANGUAGE OF ART, CRAFT AND DESIGN

Developing visual perception

Vision provides so much of the raw material for learning. What we learn is bound up with what we see. More than this, being able to see the world delights us and informs us, it moves us and enriches our lives. The visual world and our perception of it are fundamental to how we think, act and feel.

It is therefore surprising that more classroom time is not devoted to teaching which is aimed at developing a visually perceptive child. Children could be helped to understand how they see the world just as they are helped to learn how to read and write.

One of the problems for teachers is that young children need to find a plethora of forms in which all their thoughts and feelings, and perceptions of the world can be expressed. Developing visual perception at Key Stage 1 will empower children as bit by bit the richness of the visual world, as well as the huge variety of possible visual responses, are opened up. This book suggests practical classroom strategies for the simple and effective development of children's visual perception. The visually perceptive child has so much more to talk about, write about, record, contrast and compare. There is just so much more to be seen. Developing visual perception, helping children understand how they see, empowers learning and also empowers expression. It enriches the quality of being alive.

How do we see? We see the world because we can perceive certain visual qualities: shape, pattern, colour, form, space, tone and texture. These qualities (they have also been called formal elements, visual elements or visual concepts), together with line and mark, provide the chapter headings for the projects in this book. The aim is to break down the development of visual perception into an easy to manage and practical structure for the primary school classroom. Teachers will see immediately that each session links to learning in other areas of the curriculum.

The visual language of art, craft and design

Thinking visually helps children to make art, craft and design. These visual qualities can be used to focus children on the appearance of an object, a landscape or a person. This means they will know what to look for when they are drawing. The children will also recognise these same qualities in an art, design or craft object. Artists, craftworkers and designers manipulate these visual qualities as they work. Children will learn to manipulate them in similar ways as they experiment with new materials and techniques. These visual qualities become the formal elements of a visual language of art, craft and design.

A language for the expression of ideas and feelings

If young children are to have more choice about the means they choose to express themselves, they will need to be systematically introduced to a wide range of possible ways of working. The best way to achieve this is to let children explore, experiment and investigate these ways of

working for themselves. In order to do this children need clear practical structures within which to work and their teachers need a framework within which to teach. Visual perception and the visual language of art, (together with a description of a number of different processes), provide teachers with a possible framework from which to plan a wide and challenging variety of art activities.

When children can manipulate a visual language then they are empowered to express ideas and feelings. In each of these examples the formal elements become the means of expression: the light of a dark and brooding sky; a monster with a jagged form; an empty beach; a bright and cheerful pattern made up from 'higgledy piggledy' shapes; an animal with soft, cuddly fur; a red and angry face; the shape of a body curled up to hide; a jumble of tangled lines.

This book shows that it is possible and desirable for teachers to help children develop their visual perceptiveness as soon as they start school. This work builds a visual language for both an increasingly sophisticated exploration of the world around and the expression of ideas and feelings. All children have the right to be able to use art to communicate, art is not just for artists.

ART IN THE NATIONAL CURRICULUM

Art means art, craft and design

In the National Curriculum art means art, craft and design. This encompasses a vast range of activity. Artists, craftworkers and designers are concerned with: hairstyles, gardens, fashions, interior decoration, gift wrapping, baskets, ceramics, weaving, architecture, household appliances, public sculpture, furniture, cars, motorway bridges, road signs, book covers, paintings, book illustrations, pottery, scientific illustrations, telephones and much else. It is clear that art, craft and design surrounds us all our lives. Any of these areas could prompt an art activity in the classroom.

The Attainment Targets

In England the Attainment Targets are:
1. Investigating and Making
2. Knowledge and Understanding

In Wales they are:
1. Understanding
2. Making
3. Investigating

In both cases the principle is that making art becomes meaningful when it is set in context. The contexts can be investigations of the natural and made world; children's observations, memories and imagination; art, craft and design from the past, the present, our culture and other cultures. The National Curriculum implies that children and teachers will be talking a great deal. It also implies that much of the work will be experimental and explorative and that this will need to be valued. Making end products is important, but only as a part of a process.

Understanding art, craft and design

This is a feature of the National Curriculum in Art. The principle is that if children look at and talk about art they will come to understand more about their own art as well as the work of others. They will become aware of the breadth of art, craft and design and grow to understand how different examples have come to look the way that they do. This will influence and inform the art that they make themselves and it will spur them on to explore new ideas and ways of

working. Looking at and talking about art, craft and design made by others gives children a chance to make judgements and develop opinions. They will go on to make comparisons between examples of art, craft and design and their own work.

Knowledge about art

At Key Stage 1 it is enough for children to be introduced to and begin to identify different examples of art, craft and design. Through this they will begin to use an appropriate vocabulary. As you talk about art you will naturally introduce the words children need to use; at Key Stage 1 it will be words such as portrait, texture, printing, coiling, landscape, design etc. In all the examples in this book vocabulary is introduced in the context of the children working in the classroom.

Children will need to gain knowledge about the different processes involved in making art. For example, they will need to know which tools, materials and equipment are needed for what they are doing and how to use and take care of them. Again this knowledge will develop naturally as teachers introduce and then talk to children about the activity. Structured ways of introducing children to a number of different processes are included in this book.

As children become more used to looking at the work of adult artists they will develop an understanding of how artists work and be able to apply their knowledge to their own work. In practice this may mean that children see that a painter has used a whole range of different colours to make a painting. They will come to understand that artists usually need to mix colours to make paintings and go on to apply their knowledge about colour mixing to their own work. Children will also enjoy learning the names of some of the artists. They will recognise their work, learn a little about where and when they lived, how they made their art and why they made things in the way that they did.

Some activities like drawing might happen every week, even every day, others much less frequently. Some of these processes might be tackled individually, others by children working together. There is no advice or guidance within the National Curriculum orders on which to adopt other than to suggest that there should be a broad and balanced programme. This book contains examples of nearly all these processes. The index on page 86 will help you to find examples of the processes in the book.

Teachers are asked to help children understand the visual language of art, craft and design. This was explained in the previous section on developing visual perception and the visual language of art, craft and design. The point of making art is that children can have and express ideas and feelings. These ideas are generated from the context of observation, memory and imagination, from talking about art, craft and design

and from investigating the natural and made environment.

Investigating

Children will need to be visually perceptive in order to investigate the visual world and express visual ideas. Developing visual perception is essential not only to Art but to English, Science, Maths, indeed all the other areas of the curriculum. So much of what we learn is bound up with what we see. A structure to help develop visual perception provides the framework for this book.

Investigating provides the initial ideas which children can use to go on and make art. They can explore the natural and made world, and experiment with materials. Children can use their memories and imagination to generate new ideas. More than anything else, investigation implies exploring and experimenting, it allows for curiosity, trying out new ideas and for surprises.

Making art

Although the National Curriculum does not tell us which specific art, craft and design processes to teach or which specific skills children need to develop, there are some basic processes that underpin art activities:

- Making careful drawings from observation.
- Rough drawing and sketching.
- Making design drawings.
- Experimenting with materials and techniques.
- Using a sketchbook or an ideas book.
- Working in colour with pastels, crayons, pens etc.
- Working in colour with paint.
- Using clay.
- Printing.
- Collaging.
- Constructing.
- Working with fabrics and threads.
- Using a computer to aid design.

A FRAMEWORK FOR PLANNING AN ART, CRAFT OR DESIGN PROJECT

The principles of Understanding, Knowledge, Investigating and Making should not be considered separately when planning art, craft and design projects for the classroom. Throughout this book, the sequence of activities in the examples typically follows a structure. In its simplest terms this structure is about talking and doing, where talking is not confined to talking about art but is also intrinsic to helping children understand how to see. Talking also supports children as they explore, experiment and make. The model that follows is an ideal form of the process that might be followed in the classroom. Talking about examples of art, craft and design is both a pivotal and flexible component as you may want to use this to start or finish a project.

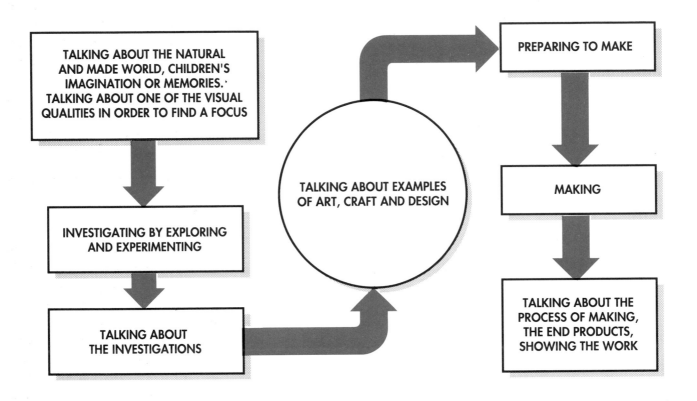

TALKING ABOUT THE NATURAL AND MADE WORLD, CHILDREN'S IMAGINATION OR MEMORIES. TALKING ABOUT ONE OF THE VISUAL QUALITIES IN ORDER TO FIND A FOCUS

INVESTIGATING BY EXPLORING AND EXPERIMENTING

TALKING ABOUT THE INVESTIGATIONS

TALKING ABOUT EXAMPLES OF ART, CRAFT AND DESIGN

PREPARING TO MAKE

MAKING

TALKING ABOUT THE PROCESS OF MAKING, THE END PRODUCTS, SHOWING THE WORK

Such frameworks are useful as examples but art cannot always be programmed in this way. Many of the activities described in this book only loosely follow this pattern. There are many possible variations. There is however, an underlying need to break down the sequence of activities into small and easy to manage units of work. This should help children build depth and quality into their art.

SOME QUESTIONS AND ANSWERS ABOUT USING THIS BOOK

What is the significance of the chapter headings?

The book is divided into eight practical sections: Shape, Pattern, Colour, Form, Tone, Space, Texture and Line and Mark. There is an index to cross reference ideas and help you quickly find particular processes and themes that you need. The practical sections reflect the emphasis on developing visual perception and the language of art, craft and design and the chapter headings correspond to the visual qualities described on page 7. These headings have been used within art education for many years and are very familiar to art specialists as the formal elements. This book applies these visual qualities (or formal elements) to the teaching of children from Reception. If we are to develop visual perception and a visual language with all the accompanying benefits for learning as a whole, we must start at the beginning as soon as children enter school.

Why is the text written in such a particular style?

There are three main voices running through the text. Firstly there is the voice of the book, setting the scene, giving hints and advice about the practical processes and commenting on what might happen. For example:

We are going to teach children a process that will help them to glue without getting in too much of a mess. When they have had some practice they will be able to make some imaginative collages.

Secondly, there is the voice of the teacher talking to the children. The aim is to phrase the questions and comments teachers might make in a way that gives an atmosphere of the classroom, as well as giving clues about how to start off the activities. For example:

"I am going to tear this paper to make an edge. Watch. What does the edge look like? How did I make the edge? Could anyone think of a way of tearing a really rough looking edge? Come and show everybody your idea. **"**

Thirdly, there are guidelines about the materials and equipment that will be needed. For example:

- Use A3 paper.
- Soft pencils, black wax crayons or notewriters.

Occasionally there are comments from children that illustrate the way they talk about investigative work. For example:

"looks like scales on a snake's skin...like a piece of toast"

Can I just dip into the book?

The book is not intended to be read through in one sitting. Dip into the pages to get a feel for the way the ideas might work in the classroom. Use the index to hunt out particular themes or processes. It would then be useful to read through a sequence of sessions to see how one session can build on another.

Is there a progression from chapter to chapter?

There is no intention to describe a progression from chapter to chapter. Conversely it would be a mistake to try and implement all the ideas at once.

So where should I start?

If you teach children in Reception or Year 1 or if you have never worked in this way before, I recommend you begin with the early sessions of the chapters on Shape, Colour, Pattern, Tone, Line and Mark, Texture, Form and Space in that order. Other combinations could also work well.

For example, schools could decide to concentrate on colour and get that working for each year group before moving on to another section.

Is there a progression from session to session through each chapter?

There is a progression implied in the way the sessions unfold through each chapter. This is in part linked to the project structure outlined on the facing page. This progression is not cast in stone. If you are working with older, more advanced children, it might be tempting to skimp on the talking and investigative work and get straight on with making something. Please do not do this. To avoid repetition modify the language and initial stimulus to accommodate the needs of more advanced pupils.

Do I need to work through every session in each chapter?

The activities in each chapter do build one upon another, but there is no need to stick to the order in a rigid way. Planning a sequence of activity that builds depth and quality into the art is a recommendation implicit throughout the pages of this book. The flow diagram on the facing page shows the importance of including a number of different explorative and discursive activities that lead up to making art. Why not design your own series of lessons to suit the needs of your children?

At what age could children be expected to try each session?

You will notice that there is no recommendation as to whether a session is appropriate to a particular year group. If older children have never worked in this way before, then all the sessions are appropriate providing the language of delivery is modified. Although the content of this publication is aimed at Key Stage 1, Year 6 children new to this way of working would move very quickly through the sessions. There should be a correspondingly rapid improvement

in their investigative and making abilities. In contrast I am constantly surprised by what children in Reception can achieve if art activities are broken down into small, easy to understand units of work as the text suggests.

How long does each session last?

Roughly one quarter of the teaching day although inevitably this is a very approximate guide.

Do I need special materials or equipment?

Everything that you may need is listed with each project. Throughout the text you will find references to drawing boards. These boards are made from thin plywood and cut to the size of at least A2 paper. They are not heavy. They will need to be sanded and if possible varnished. You will need enough for the largest class in the school. They can then be shared from class to class. These boards allow children to work outside, in the hall, on the floor of the classroom or corridor. They are invaluable for creating extra space and allowing the children to enjoy an individual working area.

Where can I find appropriate examples of art, craft and design to use when talking about art with the children?

There are many ways of providing the necessary resources. For example, use the commercial packs that are on the market and often advertised to schools; collect reproductions and photographs from colour supplements and magazines; collect postcards and birthday cards; buy posters; write to galleries and ask to be put on their mailing list for posters and invitation cards; visit a gallery with the class; organise a visit by an artist to the school; bear in mind that design covers a very broad area indeed and if appropriate include examples such as landscaped gardens, hairstyles, motorway bridges, book covers, knitted fabrics and so on.

One way of deciding what to buy or bring in to show the children would be to think about which of the visual qualities is clearly shown in the example you are considering. For example, the portrait on page 65 clearly shows light and dark and provides a focus for discussing tone with the children. You could organise boxes or files that contain good examples of art that exemplify shape, pattern, colour, form, space, tone, texture or line and mark. An alternative is to organise your collected examples by theme or topic.

In the appendix I have listed the examples of art, craft and design that were actually used by teachers in the projects that were documented.

Do the projects fulfil the requirements of the National Curriculum in Art?

The art orders can be very broadly interpreted and for that reason the text contains no specific reference to programmes of study and attainment targets. All the chapters fulfil the requirements of the National Curriculum in so many ways that it would be very repetitive to make lists of the statutory programmes of study. Good art practice should naturally and effortlessly meet the demands of the National Curriculum.

Are there examples of cross-curricular opportunities in the text?

Most of the work is cross-curricular in one way or another. The use and development of language is a recurring feature throughout the text. Some teachers may feel that the activities described in the book are worth the investment of time simply for the benefits to language development. Here are some more ideas about cross-curricular opportunities:

The work in the chapters on Shape and Form can link strongly with Maths, as can the work in the chapter on Space which will help children learn terms that describe position. The

early part of the Pattern chapter also teaches children about repeating patterns.

The chapter on Texture links strongly with an exploration of materials in Science. Link the chapters on Colour and Tone with Science. Children can learn about colour, light, shadows and so on.

Look at the chapter on Line and Mark for links with music and movement.

All the advice on drawing, which occurs throughout, will help children record. This supports investigations of the natural and made environments.

Use the index to identify examples of how the activities in the book link with specific themes and topics.

Does the book describe a complete system?

No, this is only a taste of what is possible. I hope that the text and photographs will prompt teachers to think up numerous other ways of developing visual perception and building the language of art, craft and design.

What is included in the index?

As well as themes and topics, the index lists specific examples of visual stimuli used throughout the various chapters. It also lists art, craft and design processes, examples of a basic subject vocabulary and a general listing of terms used in the text. There is also an appendix that lists all the materials and equipment referred to at the end of each practical activity and references for the works of art visible in the photographs.

Are the ideas suitable for children at nursery?

Look at the sessions in each chapter that are concerned with exploring and experimenting (leave out the chapter on Space). These can be easily adapted for work with nursery age children.

What about Reception classes?

Much of the text is written with Reception children in mind, they also feature frequently in the photographs.

As each chapter progresses some of the sessions tend to become rather involved, but I am constantly surprised by how much children in Reception will be able to do, especially towards the end of the school year.

What about Key Stage 2?

Much of the content of this book provides a starting point for children at Key Stage 2 as well. I hope teachers of children at Key Stage 2 will also find this book very useful.

When this foundation for visual perception and the visual language of art and design is in place, children will have an enormous potential means to express ideas and feelings. In other words, work at Key Stage 2 should continue both to build on the approach shown in this book and increasingly open children to their creative and expressive potential. This should mean that they will be empowered to tackle a wide range of issues with a depth and breadth of feeling.

INTRODUCTION 13

SHAPE

• • • • • Session 1 • • • • •

Talking about shapes

❝ Look around the room. Can you see any shapes? Let's make a list of the shapes you can see. Who can see a shape that is bigger than I am? Who can see a shape that is smaller than your hand? ❞

Children will immediately think of the shapes they have learnt in Maths. The first step here is to link the shapes they know about through Maths with the shapes of different things they can see in the room. If they have not yet learnt about squares, rectangles and so on, start with the next activity, drawing around objects and shapes to make outlines.

Drawing around shapes and finding out about outlines

❝ Look. Here is a shape from the shape tray. I can draw a line around this shape. This is an outline. I can find the outline of all sorts of things. What shall I try next? A spoon? A key? Let's try a few more.

These outlines make shapes. Look at the shapes we have drawn. What can you recognise? We can recognise an object by its shape. Now you can draw around more things to make some shapes of your own.❞

After you have made a few outlines with the children ask them to collect some more on their own. Provide a collection of interesting objects. Or the children could hunt around the classroom and discover shapes for themselves. Afterwards they could try and guess the objects that go with the outlines that other children collected.

- Use a large sheet of paper on an easel to demonstrate drawing around shapes.
- The children will need A4 paper and clipboards or sketchbooks to collect their own outlines.
- Soft pencils, small black wax crayons or notewriters make good clear outlines.

Finding shapes by looking

The children have been drawing around objects to make shapes. The next sequence of activities should help them collect different outlines by looking and drawing.

" I want to collect the shape of the large window in the classroom. What are the problems? Can I put the window on my paper and draw around it? Why not?

Look. If I close one eye and point at the window I can trace around the outside of the frame to draw a shape in the air. Let's all practice.

Now here is a black wax crayon. I can look at the window and instead of tracing around the frame with my finger in the air I can draw the shape with the crayon on the paper. This time I am using a crayon not my finger and I am drawing on the paper not in the air. I have to look carefully at the shape of the window.

Look at the shape I have drawn. Now you can collect the shapes of anything you want to. Just look carefully and trace around the shape in the air with your finger and then draw the outline on the paper. Let's try and draw the shape of this teapot together.

Tell me some of the other things in the room you could find outline shapes for. "

Collecting shapes by looking and drawing

" Now you can hunt around the classroom and collect different outlines by looking and drawing. See how many you can collect. Don't draw too much detail inside your shape, it's the outline that's important. "

The children could collect shapes of things much bigger than they are or they could look out of the window and collect shapes of things outside. The children should look carefully but at the same time not worry about making mistakes. The important thing is that they are looking at and drawing shapes. If they make attractive drawings that is a bonus. Soon they won't need to trace the shapes with their fingers they will just look and draw.

Talking about the shapes you have collected

" Who found an outline shape of something very large in the room or something very small..? Who found an outline shape with straight lines...with curves...? Who found an outline shape with bumps...points...?Who found..? "

Shape collections (Reception)

- Use A4 paper and a clipboard or sketchbooks.
- Try a notewriter, black wax crayon or soft pencil.
- The best drawing media for this should make a good clear dark line.

• • • • • • Session 2 • • • • •

Making collections of different categories of shapes by sorting

"On one piece of paper draw all the shapes that you have found of things that are bigger than you are.

On another sheet draw all the shapes that you have found with points."

There are many other ways of categorising shapes. The children could work on large sheets of paper and make these collections together.

Inventing large shapes

Draw a large shape with the children first so they can see the idea.

Ask the children to suggest different kinds of lines that could be used to make up the outline. A curved line, a straight line, a line with bumps, a line with sharp points and turns. Look at page 78 for ideas about working with line. They could then work together and draw some large shapes.

"You have made some large shapes. What do they remind you of? What can you see in your shapes?"

"Dots...stars...circles...a bird with a very big mouth...a pelican...a snowman's nose...teeth..."

- Use large sheets of paper off a roll.
- Marker pens make strong clear lines.

What shapes can your body make?

"When we are doing different things our bodies make different shapes. Have you any ideas about what you could pretend to do?

How about curling up and pretending to sleep? Stretch out on tip toe to reach for something high. Dig a sandcastle. Catch a beach ball. Push against a table. Tug of war with a friend. Look very sad and lonely. "

You could work from a theme such as "What do you do at the seaside?" or "What do you do in the playground?" or "Different feelings". The children will have more ideas than many adults. It is great fun asking them what they are going to do, freezing them in mid-action and talking with the class about the shape the body makes.

Collecting these body shapes

"This large piece of paper against the wall is big enough for you to draw the outline of your friend pretending to do something.

Draw around the shape of your friend slowly and carefully. Let's collect a body shape from everyone.

Now we can talk about the body shapes. Which ones are similar? Which ones look nearly the same? Which look small? Which are round? Which are long and thin...? "

In our illustration the large sheet of paper was laid out flat on the floor.

- Use a waterbased marker pen so the shapes show up clearly.
- Use paper off a wide roll of newsprint or join four smaller sheets together.

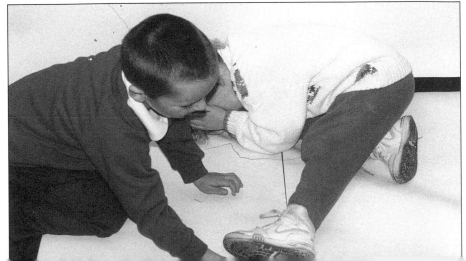

18 SHAPE

Drawing the body shapes by looking

Give each child a strip of paper divided into four.

● *Ask for one volunteer to come and make a body shape for the others to draw. The children could guess what she is pretending to do.*

● *The children should draw the first shape in the first section of paper.*

● *After they have drawn the shape they could add in anything else from memory to go with the figure. For example if the model was digging a sandcastle some children might want to add a bucket and spade etc.*

● *Repeat this three more times to fill the four sections of paper.*

Ask the children to look very carefully. They could use their fingers to trace the body shape in the air first (see page 15).

The children could choose one of their four drawings and make an imaginative painting. Perhaps their painting could show a number of people doing different things.

Talking about the body shapes in painting

"Here are two paintings. The artists have made the shapes of the people in the paintings different. What can you see in the paintings? What sort of shapes can you see? What do you think is happening? What are the people doing?"

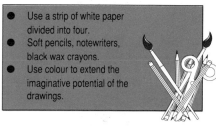

● Use a strip of white paper divided into four.
● Soft pencils, notewriters, black wax crayons.
● Use colour to extend the imaginative potential of the drawings.

Making large drawings of individual fruit and vegetables

" Everyone can choose one piece of fruit or a vegetable. Look very carefully at the shape of what you have chosen. Trace slowly around the outside with your finger. Look at all the little bumps and turns and crevices.

Here is a really large sheet of paper. You are going to make a large drawing of your chosen fruit. This will fill the paper.

So think big! Don't forget to look carefully. When you have drawn the outline you can fill in any details. "

This project helps children to be confident that they can make large drawings. It is also useful in focusing on the individual character of each separate object. For example no two carrots look exactly the same. More advanced children who have worked on texture or tones could easily add in these qualities to their drawings, see pages 64-77 .

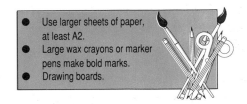

● Use larger sheets of paper, at least A2.
● Large wax crayons or marker pens make bold marks.
● Drawing boards.

Drawing a still life of fruit and vegetables

I would reserve this project for children at Year 1 or 2 who are already confident about looking and drawing. Look at page 59 and the chapter on Space for advice about helping children see how objects are positioned in relation to one another.

Include a discussion of a still life drawing or painting so that the children can look at the different shapes artists have drawn and painted.

They could make shape collections from the painting Just as they did when looking and drawing shapes on page 16. This time they are hunting for shapes in the painting rather than the shapes in the real world of the classroom.

● Use A3 paper.
● Soft pencils.
● Notewriters or black wax crayons.

Looking for shapes inside shapes

The sequence we are describing has buildings as its theme.

The first activity is a good 'warm up exercise' before making observational drawings. It will help to refocus children on shape if it has been some time since they were last thinking in that way. Look back at page 16 for ideas about helping children to look at and draw shapes.

" Who can tell us some of the things in the classroom that have large outside shapes and some smaller shapes inside them? Here are some ideas: the T.V., a large window, the door, the cover of a book. What else can you think of?

Hunt around the classroom and collect some shapes of large things by looking and drawing. Can you see any smaller shapes inside the large ones? Draw them in too. "

Talk about what the children have found. This session will work well outside.

Talking about a building

You could talk about any building in this way. Maybe there is a good, large reproduction available of architecture the children would not usually see, a historical building perhaps. But why not start with the school or the different houses, shops, factories and places of worship close by.

" Look at the front of this building. What can you see? Let's make a list of all the things you mention.

What about all the different shapes? Let's talk about all the different parts of the building that have a shape. What are the shapes like? "

You could ask the children to collect the shapes of a building as on page 16 or use the idea of collecting shapes inside shapes described in the previous section. Also you could talk about the colour and the texture of the building too.

" What is the building for? What happens inside the building?

How does the building make you feel? Is it different from where you live? Why?

Do you like the way the building looks? Or do you dislike it? What do you like or dislike about it? Why? "

- Use A4 paper and clipboards or sketchbooks.
- Any drawing media that will make strong dark lines, soft drawing pencils, notewriters etc.

Drawing a building

Use a version of this section to help the children draw any building. This is observational drawing, a study, with a focus on shape.

" We are going to look at the front of the school. First of all let's trace around the outline shape of the school in the air with our fingers. We need to be far enough away to see. What would it be like if we are too close?

Think carefully about the shape the school makes. Is it tall and fat, or long and thin? Are there any points? Any diagonal lines?

Draw the outline shape of the school on your paper. Now look carefully for all the shapes you can see inside the shape of the whole school. Draw in as many of the inside shapes you can see. Can you put the shapes in the right place?

You will need to work slowly and look carefully. Don't worry if you make a mistake just keep going. "

Another way (some would say a better way), would be to ask the children to draw the smaller shapes first, putting the large outlines in towards the end of their drawing. Ask them to start drawing in the centre of the building adding in all the shapes as they come to them.

School building (Reception)

Drawing heads and faces

The system described on the facing page works well for drawing heads and faces. Ask the children to start by drawing the eyes, nose and mouth.

As well as portraits and buildings adapt this to draw: landscapes, gardens, collections of fruit and vegetables, objects from the current topic, machines etc.

If you are working with Year 2 or older children they may worry about mistakes. They often ask for rubbers. There is a problem with some children who are so concerned about making an accurate drawing, a correct drawing, that they have no confidence to draw and are always rubbing out or asking to start again. Encourage them to keep going, everyone makes mistakes! Or ask all the children to use a notewriter, or black wax crayon so that no one can rub out.

- Use drawing boards, some A3 paper and a clip. If you are working outside use masking tape on the corners if it is at all windy.
- Use any drawing media that will make strong dark lines.

Heads (Year 1)

Bear (Year 1)

 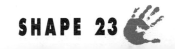

Collaging shapes cut or torn from paper

The aim is to teach the children a process that will help them to glue without getting in too much of a mess! When they have had some practice they will be able to make some imaginative collages. The project that is illustrated has 'animals' as its theme.

Cutting and tearing experiments

Ask the children to explore different ways of cutting and tearing paper.

"I am going to tear this paper to make an edge. What does the edge of the paper look like? How did I tear the paper?

Could anyone find a way of tearing a really rough edge? Come and show us. What other sorts of edges could you make? Here is one with a lot of sharp points, here is one that is wavy ...

Each of you can experiment with the scissors and with your hands, see how many different edges you can make."

- Use black paper for the tearing and cutting.
- Ask the children to lay out their edges on white paper so that they can see clearly what they have made.

The gluing process

It is so much easier for the children if they have their own individual working space. The drawing boards are invaluable here. There is a line drawn down the middle of each board to mark a boundary. There will be a clean side for the collage and a side for gluing. If the children are working on tables that wipe clean use a waterbased marker pen to delineate the working areas.

" Here is a board for you to work on. There is a line down the middle. One side is where you will do all the gluing. One side is where you will have your work.

The glue and the newspaper and the glue spreader and the damp rag must always stay on the same side of the board, the gluing side.

To start with take a sheet of newspaper and lay it on the gluing side of the board.

Here is a piece of paper with one of the the edges that you made. Lay it on the newspaper.

What happens if I put too much glue on? What happens if I put too little glue on? What happens if I only put the glue in the middle of the paper shape?

Use the spreader to put the glue around the edges of your shape. You will need to hold it steady.

Where would be a good place to put your fingers to hold the paper? In the centre!

Stick your shape down.

Wipe your hands.

Take a fresh sheet of newspaper and lay it over the first sheet.

Repeat the process to stick the torn shapes and edges on to your paper.

REMEMBER: Always put a fresh sheet of newspaper down on your board every time you glue.

Wipe your hands

Keep the glue, the spreader and the newspaper on the gluing side. "

The children can now collage the black torn and cut edges on to the white paper. They could cut and tear white paper to collage on to black. Go on to try any combination of colours for colourful experiments. Think up another way they could practice gluing.

Imaginative collages on an animal theme

Ask the children to think up different ways to colour A4 or A3 size sheets of coloured sugar paper. Use a wide range of colours. They could use soft pastels, wax crayons, anything in fact! Each child will need to colour several sheets of paper. If you use soft pastels you will need to fix the colours with firm hold hairspray before the children make the collage.

The children in the photographs had used animals as a class theme so they were full of ideas. But before trying this project the children could investigate the shapes of all sorts of different animals. Ask them to cut or tear the paper to see if they can find an animal shape!

Do not let the children draw with pencils first. Ask them to just start tearing, something will come up. Maybe you could demonstrate first. Of course the animals will be all sorts of colours and shapes.

The children could make their animal out of several shapes. They could make several animals. They could make imaginary animals.

They can glue the animals down on a clean sheet of A3 or A4 paper.

Where do the animals live? What are they doing? The children could collage more ideas or they could finish the pictures with crayons or pastels.

Use the finished work to generate stories. "Can you tell us what is happening in your collage?"

Every child will need:
- A drawing board or marked out table top.
- P.V.A., (Marvin Medium), for gluing paper or card.
- Lots and lots of newspaper cut into quarter sheets.
- Old magazines can be used instead of the newspaper. Each child will need one magazine. The children have to turn a page every time they glue.
- A glue spreader.
- Scissors.
- A damp sponge or rag for wiping sticky hands.
- Paper to make a collage on to.
- Paper for cutting and tearing.
- Coloured sugar paper cut to approximately A4 and A3 size.
- A variety of colouring media such as soft pastels and wax crayons.
- Firm hold hairspray to fix the pastels.

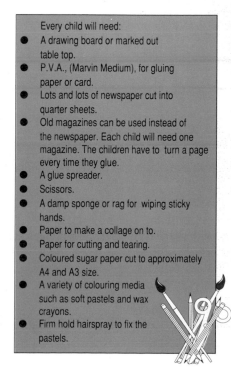

PATTERN

● ● ● ● ● ● ● ● ● ● ● ● ● ● ● ● ● ● ●

● ● ● ● ● **Session 1** ● ● ● ● ●

Repeating games

"Here is a sound. I can repeat it, I can make it again in the same way. Who can make a sound and repeat it?

Here is a movement. I can repeat it, I can do it again in the same way. Who can make a movement and repeat it? Let's all make the movement and repeat it three times.

Here are three different sounds together. I can repeat them. Who can make three different sounds together and repeat them?

Here is a shape I am drawing. I can repeat it. Who can draw a shape and repeat it three times?

Here are two colours side by side. Can I repeat them? Who can put the two colours side by side and repeat them three times? "

It is important to make the link between these repeating games and the repetition of shapes and colours that make a pattern on paper.

Talking about patterns we can see

"Look around the classroom. Who can find anything that is repeated and makes a pattern? Let's see how many patterns we can find. "

" **The counting caterpillar...the radiator...the window...Stephanie's trousers...the plastic plant pot...tiles on the wall...the candy on Hansel and Gretel's house...the computer has a pattern...**"

26 PATTERN

Drawing some simple patterns in the classroom

" Can you draw some of the patterns we talked about and any new ones you can find? When you are drawing you will have to look very carefully. "

It is better if children have done work on drawing shapes first. See pages 15 and 16.

They could also draw patterns that they can find outside.

- They could use A4 paper and clip boards or their sketch books to collect three or four different patterns.
- Use any drawing media that makes a strong clear line, soft pencils, black wax crayons, notewriters for example. The children could use colour, although to start with this can complicate the issue.

Talking about patterns in a painting

" Here is a painting, it is not the real painting but a picture of it. An artist called Matisse made the painting. What patterns can you see? Where are they? What are they like? "

"The lines on the table are curly...flowers on the wall...squiggly bits...wibbly wobbly line...it's all over....squares....like criss-cross...looks like a game...looks like wallpaper..."

Making your own pattern by drawing or painting

" Who can draw or paint a pattern of their own? Has anyone got any ideas about what they could draw to make a pattern? Try to make repeating patterns. Start at the top of the paper. Fill up all the paper with your pattern. "

If the children need help with this they could draw around shapes to make a pattern. It is better if they are free to use their own ideas.

Some children will not draw strictly repeating patterns but this is an imaginative project. The printing exercise on the following page is a more formal way of reinforcing knowledge about repeating patterns.

In the photograph children were drawing patterns that they might like to have in their bedroom at home.

Pattern collection (Year 2)

Practicing printing

You will need a collection of objects that will make prints. Try cotton reels, stickle bricks, wooden blocks etc.

● Roll out some water based printing ink on a flat plastic tray.

● Use three colours. If the children are learning about colours why not use the three primary colours?

● Put some of the objects in the red tray, some in the blue tray, and some in the yellow tray.

● Ask the children to experiment making prints on newsprint.

Making a printed pattern

Now you can reinforce the concept of a regular repeating pattern.

❝ Here are some sheets of coloured paper, choose a colour for yourself.

Choose an object from a tray of coloured ink. Make a print on the top left of your paper.

Choose a new colour and make another print next to the first one.

Which colour haven't you used? Make a third print next in line with the first two.

Now, can you repeat the order of the colours to make a colour pattern? It is hard to keep thinking of the order so keep checking your paper to decide what is coming next. ❞

Make sure there is plenty of space on the walls so that the prints can be pinned up to dry as soon as they are finished. The children will be able to see their prints clearly. Make a large display with the coloured patterns of the class. There is no need to mount the work just pin each piece close up against its neighbour until you have a large block of prints. This can be very colourful and very exciting for the children to see.

Talking about the patterns

When the patterns are pinned up the children can talk about them.

❝ Which of the patterns works really well for you? Why? Which patterns look good? ❞

● Use water based printing inks.
● Plastic trays and rollers.
● Any paper.

Investigating natural patterns

You will need to collect natural objects that show a clear pattern. Many of these patterns will be irregular. This is a good talking point.

" Look at the pattern of the orange I have cut in half. The pattern of the lines that make the grain on this piece of wood. The pattern of feathers on this bird's wing....

Why not draw the patterns you can see? Look carefully and work slowly. This kind of drawing is called a study, or a drawing from observation. "

Encourage them to fill the paper. Think big! Of course some children's natural drawing style will suggest small drawings. This requires some sensitivity to the individuality of each child.

The child in the photograph has used his investigation of natural pattern to make a print with a polystyrene tile. Turn the page for more information about printing this way.

- Use drawing boards and A3 paper.
- If the children are used to drawing with different media why not give them a choice?

Experimenting with printing using polystyrene tiles

The children can use their investigation of natural pattern to design a print that they can make with polystyrene tiles. First of all they need to find out about the process. You will need to give the children a simple demonstration. Then let them experiment to discover problems and investigate possibilities for themselves.

"On a small (8cm.sq) polystyrene tile practice using a blunt pencil to make some lines and shapes. Look at the orange cut in half for ideas. If you press too hard you will go through, too lightly and you won't see the print.

Squeeze a thin sausage of ink on to the flat plastic tray.

Roll this out with a roller to spread the ink evenly across the tray.

Put the tile flat on a half sheet of newspaper with the marked side up.

Roll some ink on the polystyrene tile with the roller. Cover all the tile. Don't forget to go over the edges.

Place the tile ink side down on some coloured paper and press flat with a clean roller.

Gently peel off the tile and look at your print.

Put a clean piece of newspaper over the inky sheet.

Use a rag to wipe your hands.

You can now repeat your print and make a pattern. Remember to get the tile the right way up. Think carefully about where it should be on the paper."

Talk about the problems with the children. They will need space to work. Encourage them to have a dirty side and a clean side to their working area. You will need storage space immediately for the wet prints. Why not pin them up for everyone to see?

- Use polystyrene tiles which you can buy from educational supply companies or use the backs of meat trays or any very dense polystyrene.
- Water based printing inks.
- Plastic trays.
- Rollers to roll out the ink.
- Clean rollers to roll over the back of the tile to make a print.
- Soft blunt pencils.
- Coloured paper.
- Damp rags.
- Half sheets of newspaper.

• • • • • • Session 4 • • • • • •

Designing a pattern to print with a tile

● *You need to decide the size of tile that each child will need to make a print.*

● *Use this as a template and ask the children to draw several adjacent tile shapes on their paper.*

● *The children can then draw ideas for their design.*

● *Ask them to try out an idea for a design in the first space. They could get ideas from the natural patterns that you collected and talked about.*

● *The children will also need to be able to look back at their drawings of natural patterns.*

● *In the photographs children were designing and printing wrapping paper.*

● *They talked about wrapping papers before coming up with ideas of their own.*

Printing the pattern

" Now transfer your design to the tile by drawing in the tile with a blunt pencil. If your lines are faint go over them again.

Now you can print a pattern. You will need lots of space. Why not work with a partner who can help you? Then you can help your partner.

You can choose a large piece of coloured paper. You will need to print your tile several times to make a repeating pattern of prints. Remember to get the tile the right way around. Remember to place it carefully next to the first print to get a regular pattern."

Is there space to pin the prints up to dry? This activity takes up a lot of room. It is very rewarding but labour intensive.

Talk about the prints the children made and the process they used. Which printed patterns look good? Which work well?

You can reinforce knowledge of the equipment and the process of printing.

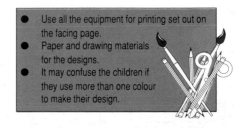

● Use all the equipment for printing set out on the facing page.
● Paper and drawing materials for the designs.
● It may confuse the children if they use more than one colour to make their design.

PATTERN AND FABRIC DESIGN

• • • • • Session 5 • • • • •

Collecting shapes or patterns

The children will be using shapes all through this project. See page 15 and 16 and the sessions on shape for ideas that will act as a warm up exercise for their explorations of pattern.

Or if the children have recently worked through the earlier sessions on pattern they could begin this project by investigating natural or made patterns in the classroom or outside. Provide a rich variety of natural or made patterns for the children to explore.

Talking about patterns in fabrics

"Here are some different fabrics I have collected. Just look at all the patterns.

Let's talk about what you can see.

We can talk about the colours and the shapes. Where can you see colours repeated? Where can you see shapes repeated? Is there anything else which is repeated?

Which patterns do you like the best? Can you say why? We could find out which pattern is the most popular."

- Use A4 paper and clip boards or sketch books.
- Use something to draw with that makes a strong dark outline, notewriters, soft drawing pencils, black wax crayons.

Drawing fabric patterns

" These fabrics have patterns. You are going to draw some of the patterns. Each group will have its own pile of patterned materials to look at.

You need only draw the pattern and only enough to show what it is like. You don't have to draw it all!

Draw the outlines of the different shapes that make up the pattern.

You will be using wax crayons, you can choose which colours you think will be the best to go with the pattern you are drawing.

You have a large sheet of paper so that there is room for at least two different patterns.

You can colour both the shapes and the background.

Don't worry about mistakes, the most important thing is that we can see a number of different patterns on your paper. "

Talk with the children about the finished drawings. Make an informal display so that the children can clearly see their work. We will be using these drawings to help them make a design.

- You could use A3 paper.
- Show the children how wax crayons make strong colours when you press hard and draw slowly. This will help them to make their pattern collections look really striking.

Talking about designing

Do the children know what design means? If not, now is a good time to introduce them to the concept.

" What would you do first to make a design for a piece of fabric? How could you plan a pattern for a fabric design? Why do you think we are going to make a design? All the fabric patterns we have seen have been designed.

To start with, an artist made a drawing to help plan the patterns we can now see in the fabric. "

Making the design

First of all show the children fabric crayons. They will use these to draw their design ideas on to some white fabric, cotton or polyester.

" We are going to use some A5 paper for our design. Look at the fabrics and look at the patterns that you drew. You can look at your own or someone else's. They are all up on the wall so that you can see them.

Use the wax crayons to try out an idea. Fill up all the A5 paper with your pattern. If you want part of your design to be white, use the white wax crayon. Have you coloured every part of your design? When you have finished your designs we will use them to help us cover this white material with colours, shapes and patterns. "

● Use A5 or even A6 paper. The younger the children are, the more difficult it will be to fill a piece of paper with a pattern.

● *Coloured wax crayons are fine. The children could experiment first to find out how they can press hard to create strong colours and lightly for paler effects.*

Choosing the designs

The project continues with the children selecting one design from the whole class to make a large piece of patterned fabric. All the designs will have to be displayed or laid out on a table so that they are easy to see.

" Have a good look at the designs. Which one do you like the best? You can talk to your friends but you must each make up your own mind. Now we can have a vote to choose the design that will be drawn on to the large piece of fabric. "

The other children can contribute their designs to make a kind of patchwork of different patterns drawn on to white material with fabric crayons. This gives every child the chance to see their own design reproduced on fabric. (See page 49)

34 PATTERN

• • • • • Session 7 & 8 • • • • •

Drawing the designs on the fabric

● *Fabric crayons are easy to use. You will get stronger colours if you let the children draw straight on to the material.*

● *Use white material, in our project three pieces were used. Two became 'patchwork' patterns using designs from the whole class. One was reserved for the design chosen by the class.*

● *It is better to stretch the fabric over a thin rectangular sheet of plywood, we used a piece 62cm x 90cm.*

● *Use a staple gun to tack the fabric on to the board. Work from the middle of each side to the corners, stretching as you go. Try to get all the creases out.*

● *Mark out A5 or A6 rectangles on to the stretched fabric. The size of each rectangle should match the children's designs.*

● *Ask each child in turn to draw their design into one of the rectangles. Bit by bit they will create a 'patchwork' of patterns.*

● *One design has been chosen. Ask the child concerned to transfer this design on to a large rectangle. He or she will need some help from other children. In the photographs Year 1 and 2 children were working on fabric 72cm x 100cm. Ideally the young designer should direct a team to transfer the design on to the fabric. Iron the fabric to fix the colours.*

Displaying and talking about the process and the product

Make a display to show all the work that was done.

“ Here are the shape collections, the patterned fabrics that I brought in for you to see, the drawings of the patterns you found in the fabrics, your designs, and the finished pieces of material. There is lots to talk about! ”

PATTERN 35

COLOUR

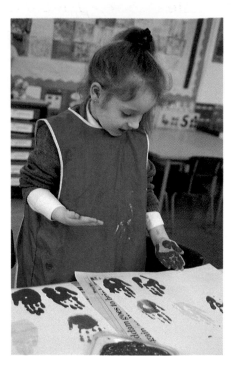

• • • • • Session 1 • • • • •

Exploring colour mixing - making hand prints

" Here is a tray of red paint, here is a tray of yellow paint, here is a tray of blue paint. Put your hand in the yellow paint. Press it on to the paper to make a yellow hand print.

Now put your other hand in the blue paint, make a blue hand print.

Now rub your hands together. What is happening? What colour are your hands? They have turned green. Magic!

Make two new hand prints with your green hands.

Now you could try the yellow and red or the blue and red.

Can you remember how to make green? "

You could call the three primary colours the magic colours. But why not introduce the correct vocabulary, primary and secondary colours? These hand prints make a great display as a frieze around the room or in a block on one wall.

One note of caution. There can be a problem mixing purples with the pigments that are usual in schools. Purple often turns out looking closer to brown. Use crimson red and a bright blue, to find a better looking purple.

- You will need some strips of paper.
- A bucket and a towel for hand washing.
- Trays of red, yellow and blue paint.
- Some help!

Exploring colour mixing - soft pastels

" We can experiment with the pastels. Look, I can put a patch of yellow on the paper. What do you think will happen if I add some blue over the top? I can mix it in with my finger. What do you think will happen if I mix the yellow and red?

Now you can try mixing any two colours together. Make good large patches. Patches not pictures! You could find out what happens when you add the white. Fill your paper with colour patches. "

Talking about colour experiments

" Which colours did you use to make this green? How about this orange? Here is a really pale red, how did you make that? Can you remember?

Do any of your colours remind you of anything? We could make a list of all your ideas. Look around the room, Which colours could you make by mixing? "

If you pin up the pastel experiments in a block they make an instant display of children's colour explorations.

Colour experiments (Year 1)

- Use soft chalky pastels. (Board chalks are weak in colour).
- Use a container for each separate colour.
- If you want the children to find a wide range of colours you will need to select two reds, two blues, a yellow and a white from the boxes.
- The pastels can be broken into small bits to share around.
- Use cheap firm hold hairspray to fix the pastel experiments.
- This will stop them smudging too much.

Talking about a painting

Ask the children to tell you about everything they can see in the painting. Make a list.

Talk about the colours.

"What colours can you see? You said you could see green, are all the greens the same? Can someone point out a dark green? How about a light green? I can see a bluey green like turquoise..."

You can build the children's colour vocabulary. The children could experiment and mix some of the colours they can see in the painting.

"How does the painting make you feel? What's happening in the painting? What would you feel like if you were there in the painting?

What do you think about the painting? Do you like it? Do you dislike it? Can you say why? Perhaps you only like some things about the painting."

Colour mixing (Year 1)

Exploring simple colour mixing using paint

" Here are the colours in the paint palette. Two sorts of red, two sorts of blue, a yellow and a white.

Here is a mixing palette.

Here are the brushes, one thick and one thin.

Here is some water.

Here is a rag.

Here is the paper you are going to paint on.

What colours do I need to make green? I can take a little yellow paint with the brush. I am putting the yellow in the mixing palette.

Now I need the blue. Now look, what will happen if I put this brush in the blue? The brush has yellow paint on it. What can I do to stop the yellow spoiling the blue in the paint palette? I can wash the brush in the water.

What's happening now? The brush is all wet and dripping everywhere. That will spoil the painting and make the table wet. What can I do? Wipe the brush with the rag. Now I have a clean brush. I can get some blue paint.

I can add this blue paint to the yellow in the mixing palette and mix them together. What do you think will happen? Now I can paint my green on the paper. I am making a good size patch.

Now I could try to mix another colour. How about orange? What colours do I need? Red and yellow, but wait, what must I do before trying to get some red with the brush? **WASH AND WIPE THE BRUSH.** You must always wash and wipe your brush. You must try to keep the colour in the paint palette clean.

O.K. Now you make a sheet of colour patches. Remember paint patches not pictures. "

Young children will often forget to paint the colours on the paper because they become so absorbed in simply mixing colours.

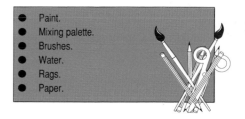

- Paint.
- Mixing palette.
- Brushes.
- Water.
- Rags.
- Paper.

Colour experiments (Year 1)

Notes about mixing colours with paint

- This is not a new technique.

- For Reception and Year 1 children try using one large plastic container of water for each group. This sits in the middle of the table. Fill it half full. It is too heavy for the children to move easily and the water will not need changing nearly so often. In this set up, an adult will have to change the water for the children.

- If the children have individual water containers they only really need to change the water when it looks like cold tea.

- Give children a thick and thin brush right from the start. As they grow older they will learn which is the best to use. It's impossible to make any small delicate marks with a thick brush alone.

- It is much better if the mixing palettes are flat. From the start this encourages children to cross mix colours they have already made.

- You can use anything that is easy to wash. The tops to freezer icecream containers are cheap and easy to collect. Encourage the children to use all available space in the mixing palette before washing it clean.

- You can use powder or readymix paint. In Reception powder can be difficult to handle but it is by no means impossible. The six well palettes are fine for holding readymix paint but small containers placed together in a tray are needed for the powder. Use yoghurt pots and a freezer size icecream container.

- A typical selection of colours would be white, bright yellow, bright blue, turquoise, bright red and crimson. Only give children the black when you are happy they are totally at ease with this process. You will need the two reds and two blues to enable the children to mix a decent range of colours.

- The rag is essential. Some teachers prefer sponges. Paper towels are not suitable.

- If you want bright colours you will need cartridge paper or even thin white card. The pigment just soaks into cheaper papers which will also buckle and crinkle when wet. However if resources are precious save your good paper for making a painting and use a cheaper kind for experiments.

Colour experiments (Reception)

● *An alternative method I have seen is to make the colour experiments on small sheets of newspaper. Ask the children to cover every inch of print in different colours. This will be very soggy to start with but is quite robust when dry.*

● *If the children are making a painting add some scrap paper for tryouts and colour testing.*

● *This process is not intended to replace other forms of painting you are already using. It is a supplement, a way of introducing young children to mixing colour.*

● *Of course there are other versions of this painting process which work well. I have found that this principle releases the children's creative use of colour, it slows them down and puts them firmly in control of what they are doing. There is no loss of spontaneity once the children are practiced at mixing colour. Year 2s, even Year 1s, say "We want to mix our colours we don't want to paint like babies."*

Exploring and recording the colours of fruit

Here is an orange, you could mix a colour for the orange and paint the orange on your paper. What about this apple, a Granny Smith, it's green all over.

Older or more advanced children could do the same again. This time peel the fruit or cut it open to reveal the colours inside. Can they add in the detail they can see? Ask them which brush is best for detail.

Use different fruits that have clear and distinct colours. Apples that are both red and green or peppers that are orange and green provide a more advanced stimulus. The aim is to make a link between the colour mixing experiments and colours that the children can see.

Here is another apple. What colours can you see in this apple? Green? Yes, but there is some red too.

Make a painting or drawing of the apple and show all the colours you can see. Here is a banana....**"**

They could record the colour changes of the fruit as it rots. Paint flowers in this way. There are other possibilities for using this method to record changes in colour for a science project.

"Remember the colour mixing experiments? You know how to mix colours. Ask a friend if you can't remember how to mix a colour.

We are not worrying about shapes here but if the children have already done work on shape this will help them. Once they get the idea they can swap fruit around and paint a line of different fruit on strips of paper. Why not add vegetables?

- You will need all the equipment for painting. See pages 39-41
- Or use soft pastels. See page 37

Still life (Year 1)

Painting a still life

- Talk about the shapes of the different fruit and vegetables. See page 15 for ideas about helping the children become more aware of shape.

- Explore the shapes by drawing as on pages 16 and 20.

- Talk about a still life painting, perhaps one by Cezanne. See page 38 for ideas about talking about a painting.

- Collect some of the colours in the painting by colour mixing. See pages 39-41.

- Talk about the still life you have made in the classroom. You may want the children to think about the way the fruit and vegetables are arranged. See page 20.

- You will need all the equipment for painting. See pages 39-41. Ask the children to mix a very pale colour in the mixing palette. They can use the pale paint to draw the arrangement of the fruit and vegetables using a thin brush. Tell them that if they think they have made a mistake they can easily hide it by painting over the pale lines. This is much better than using pencils.

- Paint is wonderful because you can paint over areas you want to change or improve. The only problem with this is that sometimes the paper gets very wet. The children will have to wait a little to let very wet areas dry.

- Encourage them to think big and fill their paper with colour. Advanced children could paint more detailed areas after filling the paper with the basic colours and shapes of the still life.

- The children could make up their own background. Patterned or plain? Simple colours or multicoloured? Leave it up to them!

- Finish off the project by having an informal exhibition. You could lay the paintings out on the tables or the floor. Talking about the finished work and looking back at earlier explorations, collections and experiments really helps the children to understand what they have been doing.

- You will need all the equipment for painting. See pages 39-41.

Still life (Year 2)

Example 2 (Year 2)

• • • • • Session 6 • • • • •

Making an imaginative painting

Spend as much time as is practical discussing the children's different ideas for an imaginative painting.

The first example is a painting of a building made after talking about impressionist paintings of Venice.

The second example was prompted by a discussion of green aliens and where they live. The third example is an imaginative "Lampton Worm" painting made after listening to the story from the North East of England.

If you have been discussing paintings, point out to the children how nearly all the artists did not leave any gaps in their work. They filled the paintings with colour.

The colour mixing slows down the painting process and allows the children to be more thoughtful about their work. The children find an increasing control over colour and the paint.

The children will need practice mixing larger amounts of paint. As they progress from Reception to Year 1 and 2 they will gradually become more and more confident.

Example 1 (Year 1)

44 COLOUR

Making a pastel drawing of a landscape

Adapt this project to fit the following themes: a garden, the nature reserve, house plants (an indoor garden).

Take the children outside to talk about the landscape, a garden etc.

" What can you see? Let's see how how many different things we can pick out. I will make a list of everything that you mention.

Now! I want you to think about all the greens you can see. Are all the greens the same? What are some of the differences? Who can tell us where they can see very dark green? What about a very pale green? Where can you see a yellowy green..? "

● *Back in the classroom ask the children to make a sheet of green colour experiments with pastels (see page 37). Ask them to remember, no pictures just patches. Some children will make a great many different greens.*

● *If the children are used to colour mixing they could use the black. They will need it to make the darkest greens. But leave the black out to start with if you feel they would use it without thought.*

● *If you are very confident about their experience with colour they could have access to all the colours in the pack. For example you could ask them to experiment and find different ways that they could change the colour of the green pastel by mixing it with different colours.*

● *Turf and natural materials make small environments in the classroom. Work from these mini-landscapes in the same way. Add some mini-beasts for excitement. Empty snail shells do not move too quickly!*

● *Talk about all the different greens the children have mixed. You could go back outside to compare the experiments with the landscape.*

● *Talk about a landscape painting. See page 38 for ideas about structuring the questions you can use.*

● *Although the focus of this example is green, in an urban or industrial environment other colours could also be explored. Other ideas for Session 7 continue over the page.*

● Use soft, chalky pastels. See page 37.

- To make the landscape or garden drawing outside you will need drawing boards. Use masking tape on the corners if there is a breeze. After all the preparation the children will have plenty of ideas about what to draw. After reminding them to look carefully, ask them to think big. Encourage them to fill their paper with all the colours, especially the greens, that they can see.

- If the weather is unsettled make sketches outside and take photographs. The children could work from these in the classroom.

- Talk about the children's work. Look at the landscape painting again. Look back at the colour experiments. Have an informal exhibition by laying the work along the floor of a corridor.

- If you display the work put up the experiments as well. It really shows the children how much you value that work too.

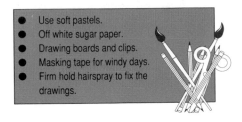

- Use soft pastels.
- Off white sugar paper.
- Drawing boards and clips.
- Masking tape for windy days.
- Firm hold hairspray to fix the drawings.

• • • • • Session 8 • • • • •

Landscape (Year 2)

Painting a landscape, a garden, house plants...

The landscape project could be easily adapted for paint. See pages 39-41 for an outline of the colour mixing process.

Linking with other visual qualities

The work on landscape drawings could be linked with the other sections of this book. Older children may well have covered some of the work on texture, space, tone, line and mark, pattern and shape.

As they become more familiar with this visual language they will instinctively combine more and more of these ideas. To start with in Key Stage 1, one concept at a time is often more than enough to handle, but more advanced children in Year 2 might be happy to think of the shape and the textures they can see as well as all those different greens.

It is not too difficult to paint outside in good weather. Use two dustbins half full of water for every fifteen children or so. One stays clean for fresh water, the other is for dirty water and rinsing palettes.

Landscape (Year 2)

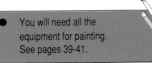

- You will need all the equipment for painting. See pages 39-41.

Imaginary landscapes

- This project begins with an emphasis on shape. The children move on to use both shape and colour.

- Talk about the shapes the children can see in a landscape or townscape.

- Ask them to explore the shapes by drawing and collecting as on page 16.

- Inside the classroom ask the children to choose five shapes of different things from their shape collections and cut larger versions of these out of paper.

- They can rearrange these shapes in any way they like on a new piece of paper. They are making a new landscape of their own. Discuss with them all the possibilities. Perhaps a tree could become a cloud, a building could become a field? They could borrow shapes from others in the group or pool all the shapes together.

- When they have an idea of where some of the shapes are going on their paper they can use them as templates to draw around.

- Use colours to complete this imaginary picture. Soft pastels are good for large areas and this can be linked to colour mixing see page 37. The children could add more imaginary details to the landscapes. Encourage them to fill up the whole paper.

- You could adapt this idea to make pictures of imaginary people, gardens, buildings.

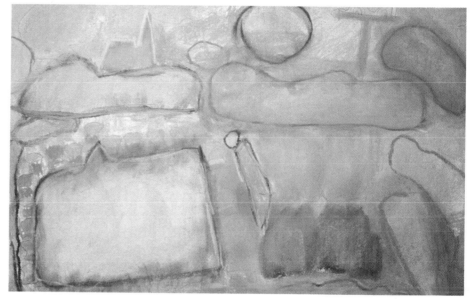

Imaginary landscapes (Year 2)

Bubbles

● *Make some colour experiments with soft pastels. See page 37. If the children have recently used the pastels perhaps you could leave this out.*

● *Talk about the experiments.*

● *Put a little washing up liquid in the bottom of a large clear bowl. Show the children how they can blow through a straw to make a mountain of bubbles.*

● *Talk about all the colours they can see in the bubbles. Talk about the bubbles themselves. What are they like?*

● *Ask the children to make drawings of the bubbles.*

● *Talk about the work that is produced.*

● Use soft pastels. Restrict the colours to two reds, two blues, a white and a yellow if you want the children to explore mixing as well.
● Use large A3 or A2 size paper. Off white sugar paper would be fine.
● Drawing boards will help create a flexible working area. Children could work on the floor. Use inexpensive firm hold hairspray to fix the drawings.

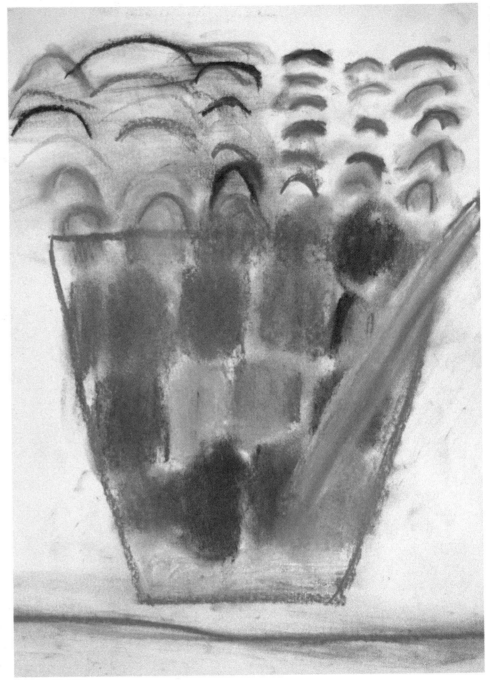
Bubbles (Year 2)

Other ideas for working in colour

Adapt some of the previous sessions in this section for other colour work. Here are some ideas: Trees in different seasons; flowers; hot and cold colours; an Ice King and Fire Queen; recording changes in colour in Science, for example changes as iron rusts.

The children could try making a colour chart for an imaginary paint company; colour in fabric design (see page 32); colours in the city; animal colours; skin tones; water; the sea; a pond; a river; buildings; bricks; stone; monsters; fashion; food; colours and moods; bonfire night; kites; balloons; parties; birds; an imaginary planet and many more.

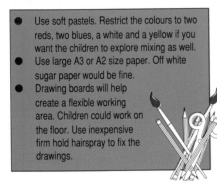

Painting at an easel with readymix paint

Earlier in this chapter we described ways of introducing children to mixing colours using paint. This process is not intended to replace other ways of painting that are already working in the classroom. For example, you may wish to introduce colour mixing whilst allowing children to continue to paint at easels with readymix paint.

Working with fabrics and thread

In this photograph children are weaving coloured wools. Working with fabrics and thread provides an alternative media for working in colour.

FORM

• • • • • • Session 1 • • • • • •

Talking about simple forms

"Here is a sphere, here is a cube. Can you see any differences between them? Here is a pyramid, here is a cone. Can you see any differences between them? Here is a cuboid, here is a cylinder. Can you see any differences between them...?

Which of these forms are curved? Which of the forms have flat sides? Is there a form that has no edges ?"

Making a simple form in clay

This is a good way to begin to use clay. You can introduce the process as outlined on the next page.

"First of all who can find a way of making a sphere? Experiment. Now try a cube...now a cylinder...now a pyramid. Keep practising until you have a set of simple forms.

Who could tell everybody how they made a sphere? What about the pyramid? Did anyone use a clay tool? How did you use it? What parts of your hands did you use...? "

Using clay

- Red earthenware is an inexpensive clay. Use buff coloured clay if you want to glaze or paint the objects bright colours. Do not mix different clays together.

- Prepare the clay in advance. For these projects use the clay straight from the bag.

- Estimate how much clay each child or each group of children will use. Put the portions of clay in plastic food bags and seal them tightly. This means you can hand out the clay to the children without everyone becoming covered in clay before they start. Tell the children not to open the bags until everyone is ready. The clay will stay moist in the sealed bags for a considerable time.

- Give each child a wooden board to work on. Some teachers prefer to have one side of the board covered in a hessian type material to prevent the clay sticking to the wood. Alternatively you could put a paper towel on the board.

- Have a selection of clay tools available, or use old cutlery, lollipop sticks etc.

- Talk about what clay is like. As the children handle the clay it will quickly start to dry out, cracks will appear, flakes will crumble off. Show the children this. They must know that the more they handle the clay the drier it becomes.

- Observing changes in clay over a period of time could be a science project. Try leaving the clay in the open air, in a paper bag, in an open polythene bag and in a sealed polythene bag. Ask the children to observe the changes that take place over a number of days.

- The fact that clay dries out when you are handling it presents a problem. Water, clay and very young children do not mix. There is a way of keeping clay just moist enough to handle.

- Have a wet, but not wringing wet, sponge in a polystyrene tray, one for each child. When the clay feels dry, or their hands are dry, the children can press their palms down on to the sponge. There should be just enough wetness so that the sponge does not drip. The children's moist hands will keep the clay in a good condition for the work.

- If you want the children to join two pieces of clay together they will need some slip, this is a clay glue made from clay and a little bit of water. Stir this around in a yoghurt pot until it becomes the consistency of thick double cream. The children will need a brush to apply the slip.

- You will have to seal any unfinished work in plastic bags if you want to keep the clay moist enough to work with from one day to the next.

- For best results you will need to fire the clay. Make contact with your local secondary school art department or try the tertiary colleges or colleges of F.E. They may help you out if you only need work fired occasionally. Glazes are a luxury. One biscuit firing will be enough. The children can seal the clay with P.V.A. (dilute it with a little water) and then paint their objects if appropriate.

- The clay can be left unfired. It will be very brittle but at least the children can see their work displayed. Shoe boxes are useful for storage as well as moving the objects around. You could get at least two objects in one box with plenty of packing. These boxes stack easily.

- Fibre clays are expensive, are not nearly as satisfying to use but do not need firing.

• • • • • Session 2 • • • • •

Talking about how to change a simple form

Use the forms that the children have made in the last session. You will also need to show them the slip and explain that they must use it like a glue if they want to join two forms together.

❝Here is a cube made out of clay. What can I do to change the cube? Here are the clay tools. How could I use these to change the cube?

How would I make a hollow? How could I make a sharp point? How could I put a hole through the cube? How could I round off the sides? Can I make it wider or taller?

What could you do to change this sphere? Why not join two forms together? We can then go on and make even more changes.❞

Experimenting with clay forms

The children could start off by making some simple forms. Two or three larger forms will be more useful than lots of small ones. They can now make their own imaginative sculpture.

❝Remember all the ideas we had for changing forms. See if you can make changes to the simple forms you have made. You could make holes, hollows, sharp edges, bumps, curves, or anything else you can think of.

Why not join two forms together? It doesn't have to look like anything you know. Just have fun making your own imaginative form.

One person might not have much clay. But if three or four of you work together to combine your ideas and clay you will be able to make something big.❞

Talk about all the different forms the children have made. Keep a note of the vocabulary for the session on talking about sculptures.

The children will now have ideas to help them model in clay. One child in the photograph spontaneously made a pair of binoculars!

52 FORM

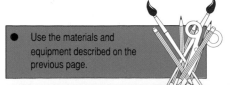

● Use the materials and equipment described on the previous page.

Talking about a sculpture

Artists who work in three dimensions use many of the qualities associated with form. Their sculptures are difficult to talk about through photographs, so much of the essential three-dimensional quality is missed. Ideally you will want to discuss actual sculpture. Have you or your colleagues any sculptural objects at home? Can you visit an art gallery? Are there any examples of public sculpture near by? Places of worship and civic buildings often have sculptures. Is there a sculptor who you could ask to visit the school? If all this is impossible then photographs are better than nothing.

"Here is a sculpture, what can you see?

Let's talk more about the form of the sculpture. Remember we have talked about the forms that you made. You made sculptures that were flat, narrow, wide, hollow, curved, rounded, smooth, sharp, thin, tall, heavy looking, feathery, holey... Could we use words like this to describe these sculptures?

Do the sculptures remind you of anything? Is anything happening? How does the sculpture make you feel? Do you like or dislike the sculpture? Have you a reason?"

• • • • • Session 3 & 4 • • • • •

Talking about objects made from clay

One way to start the project would be to look at a coiled pot made by a craftsworker. Coil pots have been made throughout history in many different cultures.

You could also discuss different objects from the home that are used to contain fluid such as vases, teapots, jugs etc. Pick ceramic items. Talk about the different forms they take and the fact they are made out of clay.

Practising making coils

This is also a good way to start to use clay. You will need all the equipment for using clay. See page 51 for detailed advice.

" Here is a thick wax crayon. Can you roll out a sausage shape that is the same thickness as the crayon?

Use the flat palm of your hand to roll. Try to make the sausage the same thickness all the way along. Keep practising. One problem is that sausages can get too thin and break.

Now here is a length of paper. Can you make the sausages the same thickness as the crayon and as long as the paper? You can use the paper to measure your sausage. You can cut the sausage if it is too long. These sausages will become our coils. Make five or six. "

The short side of an A4 sheet seems to be a good length.

- Use the materials and equipment described on page 51.

Joining the coils and making a coil pot

" Are all the coils (the sausages) the same length? Have you made five or six?

Take one coil and make it into a circle. Join the ends together. Remember to use a little bit of the slip, our clay glue. Smooth down the join.

Make a new circle. This circle will go on top of the first one. Use a little slip to glue them together. Build up the coils until you have a cylinder. Use a little slip every time you want to join two bits of clay.

Put one hand inside the cylinder and press your fingers gently against the side of the coils. Now using a flat clay tool, carefully smooth down the outer side of the pot. "

Young children, four and five year olds for example, will find smoothing down the coiled cylinder very difficult. Why not just leave it as it is?

Making a base

" Make a long coil, put it flat on the board and make it into a spiral, like a snail. Will your coiled cylinder fit on to this? Add another piece of coil to the spiral if it is too small.

Use the slip to join the cylinder to the base. Smooth down the joins. "

Scrape initials into the base to identify the pots. If the children want to decorate their pots with textures or patterns cover them with plastic and they can work on them the following day. It is better if they are slightly dry rather like stiff leather.

Talking about the problems

You will reinforce knowledge about the process by asking the children what they found difficult and what problems they had.

 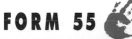

Working together to make a large coil pot

" Everyone can help to make one big coil pot. You will be working together one group at a time. There will be four in each group. Two children in the group can make the coils. The other two can build the coils into a pot. After a while you can swap jobs.

Start by making a spiral base. The size will depend on how much clay you have.

This time the coil can be any length because we are going to make our pot by making a spiral of coils, round and round, higher and higher.

You must remember to use the slip to join the ends when you add a new coil. Don't forget to use slip on the top of the pot before you add each new bit of coil. Go slowly so that it looks good.

When you have coiled the first length on top of the base keep on adding more coils.

This time don't let the pot get too big without smoothing the sides. Don't touch your pot more than you have to. Don't make the coils too thin. "

The younger the children are the more help they will need. Reception children need an adult on hand all the time. But it is amazing how much they will do on their own.

Decorating the pot

The children could decorate the pot by making marks, lines or patterns in the side. To practice ideas ask them to experiment on a small slab of clay (see page 74).

Practice with different tools and objects making marks and patterns. They could come up with an idea on paper first.

Why not use letter forms as a starting point to make patterns? Perhaps the class could decide which patterns could be used to decorate the pot.

Leave the pot to dry a little before decorating it, although it must be soft enough for the children to score the pattern on to the side.

FORM AND CONSTRUCTION

• • • • • • Session 6 & 7 • • • • • •

Talking about sculpture

Look back at page 53 for a discussion of some of the problems involved in talking about sculpture. In the photographs the children from Years 1 and 2 were visiting the Glynn Vivian Art Gallery in Swansea to take part in a project organised as part of the gallery's education programme.

Talking about materials

This project involved constructing with wire and plasticene. The wire (4.2mm gauge) was soft and very easy to bend. It was pre-cut into a variety of different lengths ranging from a few centimetres up to a metre. First the children were given a little plasticene and a length of wire to explore.

❝Play with the wire a little. What is it like? Play with the plasticene. What is that like? Tell me some of the differences between the wire and the plasticene.❞

Experimenting with the wire and plasticene

❝Can you make three pieces of wire stand up together? Try out a number of different ideas.

Now can you practice bending the wire to make some shapes.

You can make simple shapes like squares and circles but you can also make any shapes you like. Make at least four different shapes. Try to find ways of joining the shapes together to make them stand up.❞

Talking about the experiments

Ask the children about what they found easy and difficult to do. They will inevitably have encountered problems to do with balance and stability. This is a good time to introduce them to these concepts.

Making a construction

"Now you can make a sculpture of your own. Work together in groups of three. You will have to help each other all the time. See which group can construct the biggest wire sculpture. It must be stable. It's no good if it keeps on falling over.

You can use the wire shapes you have made, the wire lengths we have cut ready and the plasticene."

The children don't have to try and make anything they can recognise. In fact the most useful work will be abstract as they try to gradually build up a large and more complex structure. However some children in our project chose to make sculptures that related to familiar things. One group chose to make bridge, another a sculpture based on the art gallery.

Drawing the finished construction

The wire sculptures made excellent objects to draw. This would clearly link to work on line, look at pages 78-83 for other ideas about line.

"First of all find the point of view from which you would like to draw your sculpture. Look around the sculpture first before deciding. Look carefully at all the different lines and shapes you can see. Here is a large sheet of paper and a selection of materials to draw with. Think big!"

Some of the children naturally worked in terms of shape rather than line.

Talking about the sculptures and the drawings

The project ended with a discussion about the sculptures and the drawings.

- Use wire, pre-cut into different lengths.
- Plasticene.
- Drawing boards.
- Large sheets of sugar paper.
- A variety of coloured drawing media for making strong bold lines.

S P A C E

Teddy bears picnic (Reception)

• • • • • Session 1 • • • • •

Drawing objects one at a time as they appear on a magic table!

The children should know about drawing the outline shapes of objects. First try some of the shape exercises on pages 14-21 as a warm up and reminder. In this session you will be building children's vocabulary about space with words and phrases like 'next to', 'on top of', 'behind', 'in front of', 'between', 'underneath'... If you want to explore concepts such as in 'front of', the children will need to become familiar with the idea that shapes can overlap in their drawings.

In this example Year 1 children are drawing a teddy bear, a teapot, a ball and a bottle. The theme could be a picnic. Of course many other themes and objects could be used.

" Here is a magic table! Things are going to appear one at a time. I wonder what the first thing will be? Here it is, a teddy bear. Look where it is going to sit. I am putting it in the middle of the table. Put your drawing in the middle of your paper. Think about the shape. Draw the outline.

Now here is a teapot. Where is it going to go? Next to the teddy bear? Beside the teddy bear? On which side of of the bear is the teapot? Look carefully at where it is going on the table. Where do you think you should draw the teapot on your paper?

Here is a bottle. I am going to place it in front of the teddy bear. Look carefully, does the bottle hide part of the bear?

Can you draw the bottle so that it hides part of the bear? Where are you going to draw the bottle on your paper?

I am going to place the ball on the table. Can you see all of the ball? Is part of it hidden? You don't have to draw the parts you can't see, the parts that are hiding. "

All those who are drawing will need to be in front of the magic table so that they have the same viewpoint. There will be lots to talk about in these drawings.

- Use A3 paper and ask the children to think big!
- Drawing boards are helpful as they create extra space for the children to work.
- Any drawing media that make strong clear lines, black wax crayons, soft pencils etc.

Talking about objects near to and far away

● *Find two children in the class who are the same height.*

● *Now take the class outside.*

● *Send one of the two children about 40 metres away, or to the back of the playground.*

● *Ask the second child to stand 20 metres away, between the first child and the class.*

" We are all standing and looking at the two children. Is there a difference between them? Remember that inside we found that they were the same height. "

● *Ask the child who is furthest away to walk slowly towards the class. She should stop when she reaches the second child.*

● *Now ask her to walk forward until she is really close to the group.*

" What is happening? Are they still the same height?

What happens as she walks towards us? She seemed to get taller as she walked towards us. Let's try this again. Look how small she looks at the back of the playground.

What other things look smaller when they are further away? "

● *You have been showing children the effects of perspective. Good examples to look for are houses down the street, railings, street lights, trees, cars ...*

Drawing things near to and far away

Work outside or find a view from a window.

" We have found out that things look smaller in the distance and bigger when they are close to us.

Look carefully see if you can show this in your drawing. "

● If you are working outside the classroom the children will need drawing boards to rest on.
● If it is windy you will need masking tape for the corners.
● Use A3 paper and soft pencils, black wax crayons notewriters etc.

Note

I would recommend reserving the rest of the projects on space for children in Year 2 who are already working with confidence.

Talking about space in landscape painting

"Here is a painting, a landscape. What can you see? We can keep a note of what you say.

Which part of the painting is furthest away? What part is closest to us?

Now we can pretend to walk through the painting. We will walk through the painting starting at the front and moving into the distance. What would you pass on the way? You have magic powers and can pass through or over everything. We can make a list of everything that you pass.

Describe everything you can see in the foreground. All those things that seem to be closest to us. Now describe everything you can see in the background, in the distance. "

You could go on to ask the children about what they can see in the middleground.

Use the new words here, foreground and background. Add the word middleground if you think it is appropriate.

This could equally relate to talking about a townscape or industrial painting or drawing. Paintings of interiors often show a complicated space. In the case of an interior perhaps the children could imagine themselves as mice or ants that are walking through the space of the painting.

Talking about space in the classroom

You can talk about space both inside and outside the classroom.

"We are sitting at one end of the classroom. Can you tell me what things are the furthest away from us..?

What is close to us? What about some of the things in between? What is in front of the big table..? What is behind..? What is between the big table and the door..?"

The children could talk about the way one object overlaps or partially covers another. For example, the chair overlaps the table, in other words the chair is in front of the table.

Ask the children to experiment by drawing shapes that overlap. They could colour the new shapes that are made by the overlapping outlines.

● For the overlapping shape experiments use
   A3 or A2 paper
● A selection of coloured wax crayons or felt pens.

• • • • • Session 4 • • • • •

Talking about space outside

You are going to ask the children to take an imaginary walk through the real space that they can see. You will need to be able to see a reasonable distance either standing outside or looking from a window.

❝ What can you see that is the furthest away from us? Now imagine that you can stand there. You have magic powers and can walk right through or over everything in a straight line all the way back to where everyone is waiting.

What do you pass first of all on your walk, what do you pass next, and then? Let's make a list starting with the far away things and gradually adding the others as we pass them.

Drawing space outside

❝ Now you can draw. First of all draw the things that are furthest away. Then draw what you would pass next on your magic walk, then the next things until you are close. ❞

The children might draw one thing on top of another, building up the drawing with lots of overlapping shapes, lines and marks. If they are used to drawing only what they can see they might be able to show that one thing hides part of another. In other words not all of an object is visible, the children need only draw what they can see.

Talk about these drawings in the same way that you talked about the walk through the painting, see the previous page.

Another idea is to give the children strips of paper. Perhaps they could draw all the things they can see in the distance on one strip and those things in the foreground, on another. You could even have a strip for the middleground! Ask the children to combine the strips in one new, large drawing.

- ● Use A3 paper or sketchbooks.
- ● Are the children able to choose their own drawing media? Some will prefer charcoal, others soft pencils etc.

Making a 3D model of an imaginative space

- *Prepare strips of card.*

- *Ask the children to think of an imaginary planet.*

- *What would they see in the distance? For example, what would they see in the sky? Ask the children to talk about their ideas.*

- *They could then make drawings with marker pens or coloured wax crayons. Ask them to fill their strip of card with the ideas and the colours that they will see in the distance when they are standing on the imaginary planet.*

- *Ask them what they would see in the foreground. Let them share some more ideas. They can draw their ideas about the foreground on a second strip of card.*

- *On the third strip the children can draw their ideas for the middleground.*

- *The three strips they have drawn will make a model of a view on the imaginary planet. They can bend or cut the strips, or they could cut things out of the foreground and middleground strips. They could also cut spaces in these strips so that they can see through them to the background.*

- *Ask the children how they can make the strips stand.*

- *Talk about and display the finished models.*

- *The children can easily work together to talk about and make the models.*

- *You could adapt this idea to help children design stage sets or box theatres.*

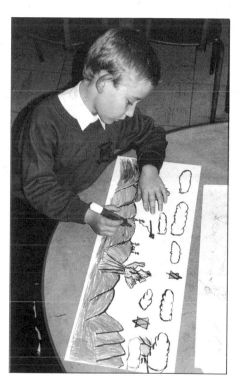

- Use cardboard cut into strips.
- Coloured marker pens and wax crayons if you would like strong clear colours.
- Scissors.
- Glue and scrap card might be needed to make tabs etc.

TONE

• • • • • Session 1 • • • • •

Talking about light and dark

❝ There are some dark places in this classroom. Where are the darkest places? Look around. Why are these places dark? How could we make them lighter?

Where are the lightest places in the room?

Where can you see shadows? Look for shadows. How can we make a shadow? ❞

Take the children into a room that you can black out. Talk about what it is like in the room and then let some light in. They will be learning that they need light to see. If you cannot find a dark room then simply close the blinds or curtains in the classroom.

Ask the children to experiment by making shadows.

Link the discussion of light and dark with memories and feelings, for example:

❝ Have any of you been anywhere where it is really dark? Lets make a list of dark places. What are they like? How did you feel? ❞

Experimenting with light and dark

❝ Here is some charcoal and some chalk. Which one would you use to make a dark patch? Which one would you use to make a light patch?

You can experiment and make some dark and light patches on your paper. What happens when you mix the charcoal and chalk together? ❞

Ask the children to make patches of light and dark. Show them a patch of charcoal and say "no pictures just patches." You will need to reinforce this from time to time while the children are working.

Talk about all the different greys the children find. Ask them to talk about the different shades of grey and how they made them.

It is important to let the children talk about their experiments.

The drawing boards will be very useful here. They will help you find extra space in the classroom so that all the children can experiment at once, some will be able to work on the floor.

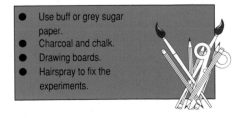

- Use buff or grey sugar paper.
- Charcoal and chalk.
- Drawing boards.
- Hairspray to fix the experiments.

64 TONE

Making a tonal scale

You could introduce the word tone here, use terms like the darkest tone, the lightest tone...

A good way of helping Reception children understand this idea quickly is to talk about hair tones.

" Who has the darkest hair in the class? Has anybody got really black hair? Let's choose the person with the darkest hair.

Who has got the lightest hair in the class? Is there anyone who is really blonde. Let's choose the person with the lightest hair.

Let's choose two more children, one who has lightish hair and another one who has darkish hair. I will help you choose. "

The children can now decide which order the four children should stand in to show a progression from dark to light tones.

" Now we could use the charcoal and chalk to make a tonal scale. Start on one side of the paper with a dark patch put a very light patch on the other side. Make patches of grey tones that go from dark to light. "

Challenge the children by increasing the number of patches in the tonal scale.

If you are working with older children you could try all of session 1 with a range of different drawing media. The children could experiment with soft pencils. black wax crayons etc. If the children can mix colours they can make tonal experiments and scales with black and white paint or different colours. See page 39-41 for advice about colour mixing.

- Use strips of buff or grey sugar paper.
- Charcoal and chalk.
- Hairspray to fix the tonal scales.

• • • • • Session 2 • • • • •

Talking about light and dark in a drawing or painting

Find a reproduction of a drawing or painting where the artist has clearly used shadows and a variety of tones. Start by asking the children the question "What can you see?"

" I am going to make a list of all the things that you can see in this painting. Let's not leave anything out... "

Encourage the children to state the obvious!

" Now let's look at the tones. Where are the darkest parts? Where are the lightest parts? How did the artist make those areas so dark? How were the lightest tones made? Let's look for shadows. "

Now try asking questions like:

" What is happening in this painting? Does the painting remind you of anything? How do you feel when you look at this painting? Why? How are the people in the painting feeling? What are they like?

What is it you like about this painting? Why? What is it you dislike about this painting? Why? Maybe some of you like this painting more than others. "

You can talk about the drawings and paintings the children make in this way too.

" What kind of man do you think he is? "

"Nasty, mean, cruel, he looks mad, his mouth looks mad and cross, he's looking at us."

Drawing light and dark

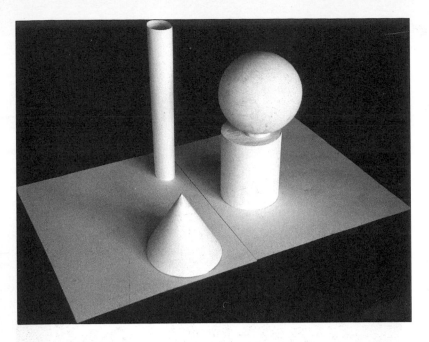

You can use some very simple white forms, a cylinder made from a roll of white paper; a sphere (use a white ball); a box painted white; a large paper cone. Put them on some white paper and use a lamp or spotlight to make shadows. Have the children experimented by making simple forms in clay? Look back at page 50 and 51 for ideas.

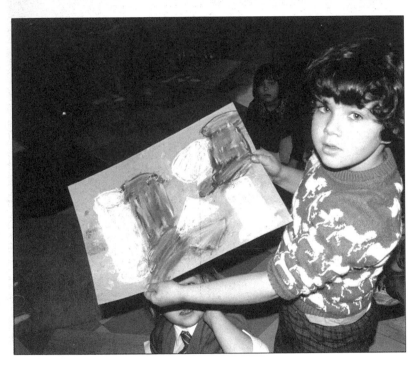

"What's happening here? Lets talk about the shadows. Look very carefully. Can you point to the darkest shadows of all? Now, who can show me the lightest parts?

Make a drawing with the chalk showing the lightest parts of the forms first. Then add the darkest parts with the charcoal. You could try mixing the charcoal and chalk for some of the other shadows. "

Try shining the light from the other side and asking the children to make a second drawing.

"Let's talk about the drawings. What did you find easy? What was difficult? Look at all the drawings. Can you choose one that you like? Can you choose one that you think works well? "

Have an informal exhibition by laying all the work out in the corridor or on the floor and table tops in the classroom.

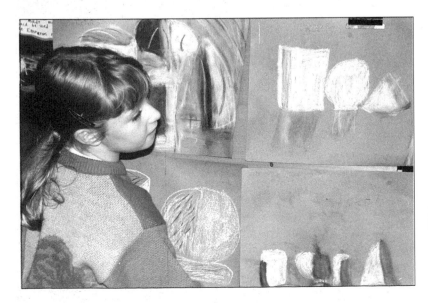

- Use charcoal and chalk.
- Buff or grey sugar paper at least A3 size.
- Inexpensive firm hold hairspray to fix the drawings.

Recording shadows

"When it's sunny our bodies make good shadows on the ground. How could we record these?"

You could use a camera, or the children could draw around the shadows on large pieces of paper.

Ask the children to record the shadows they make when they are doing different things, for example: sitting, standing, reaching, running, standing on one leg, making a star shape. Make a link with the body shapes project on page 18.

You could record the shadows that other things make, such as a chair or a toy...

Exploring light sources

"Let's make a list of all the things that you can think of that give off light. Here are some things that I have collected to show you, a torch, a candle, an oil lamp, an electric light... a diva

What is the light like that comes from the torch? What kind of light comes from the candle? I am going to make a list of all the words we are using.

Let's look at the different shadows that we can make with these things.

Now, who can pretend to be a torch? Who can pretend to be a candle...?

Now you can make some drawings of the different objects that give off light."

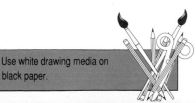

● Use white drawing media on black paper.

TONE 67

Drawing a portrait looking for tones

- *Ask the children to make experiments with light and dark as on page 64. They could use different drawing media to explore light and dark and afterwards make a choice about what they would like to draw with.*

- *Talk about the experiments.*

- *In this example I will assume that the children are going to draw each other. But the project would work well for any portrait.*

- *Ask the children to find partners.*

"Look at your partner's head. Where can you see the darkest parts of the head? Where can you see the lightest parts? Where can you see shadows?

We have been experimenting with different drawing materials making light, dark and grey patches.

When you draw look for the dark and light areas and look for the shadows. Draw carefully and put in whatever you can see.

Don't draw the outline first but pick a spot in the middle somewhere, start there and work towards the outside of the head. This means that you will probably start with the nose or the eyes or the mouth.

Just keep going and don't worry about your mistakes.

When you have finished we can talk about the drawing."

A useful tip for children is that the eyes are half way between the top of the head and the chin.

Adapt this project in order to draw buildings, landscapes, a cityscape, or a still life of objects connected with a topic.

- You will need drawing boards and clips.
- If you are using charcoal the children will need large sheets of paper. Try at least A3.
- The children could use a variety of drawing media choose paper that is appropriate.
- For example, buff sugar paper for charcoal and chalk.

68 TONE

Portrait (Year 2)

Making imaginative drawings using light and dark tones

There are many novels or stories that have passages concerned with the effects of light or of darkness. For example, "Who's Afraid of the Dark?", by Crosby Bunsul or "The BFG", by Roald Dahl.

" Listen to this part of the story...

Close your eyes, use your imagination and think about a dark place of your own. Is it a cave or is it night time? Is it in the attic or in a cellar? Where else could you be? What else is there?

Make a drawing of the darkness.

Add in anything you like that will show us what is there. "

● *If the children have not explored tone for a while, repeat some of the sessions earlier in this chapter to warm them up.*

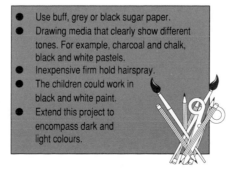

● Use buff, grey or black sugar paper.
● Drawing media that clearly show different tones. For example, charcoal and chalk, black and white pastels.
● Inexpensive firm hold hairspray.
● The children could work in black and white paint.
● Extend this project to encompass dark and light colours.

TEXTURE

• • • • • Session 1 • • • • •

Talking about texture

Ask the children to feel materials like bricks, feathers, stone, moss, tree bark....

❝Here are some things we have collected. They all feel different from one another. They all have different textures. If you could touch this one what would it feel like?

Now touch it with your hands. Tell me what the texture really feels like. I am going to make a list of all the words you have used to describe the textures.❞

Experimenting with marks to make textures

The children will say that the textures feel rough or smooth or feathery, some are soft, others are spikey etc.

They are now going to experiment. Can they draw marks that correspond with the textures they have discovered? They will not be drawing pictures. Start off by trying this out with the whole class or group so that every one can see the idea.

❝To start with let's use the black wax crayon. I am going to make a mark that I think looks rough. Could somebody come up here and make a mark

that looks rough. Could somebody come up here and make another rough looking mark? Does that look really rough? Who can make an even rougher looking mark? Now we could try a soft mark...

Now you can try and make marks of your own. How about marks that are very feathery? How did you make that mark? Now we could try marks for a bumpy texture. Could any of you think of a new texture to try? Remember our list. Remember, just experiment, you don't need to draw a picture.❞

After talking about the materials and textures try hiding the objects away while the children are drawing. You could use feely boxes.

Texture Experiment (Year 2)

Talking about the texture experiments

"Look at your drawing experiments. What are these textures? What do they look like?"

"Sponge...crumpet...it's softer than the other one...looks like a towel, it has little bits of cotton that stick up to dry you....looks like the scales on a snake's skin...like a piece of toast, yes burnt toast! Looks like the bark of a tree where a woodpecker has been pecking... looks like a beard a bit."

- Use strips of paper if you want the children to store the marks one after another.
- Or an A2 sheet of paper divided into two.
- Try charcoal, wax crayon, soft pencils.

Hunting and collecting textures outside

" Hunt around the play ground and find as many different textures as you can.

Do you remember the different marks you made to go with all the textures? Can you draw the textures you have found? Don't draw the things, just draw the textures. You don't need to draw a picture, just make some marks to go with the texture.

Now we can make a collection of things that have different textures and bring them back to the classroom. "

Teachers and children can use cameras to collect the textures of different surfaces.

You could look for the textures inside.

Visit the beach, some woodland, a builder's yard. This project links well to an exploration of materials in the natural and made environment.

It is important to talk about the textures the children have drawn and collected.

The experiments, drawings, photographs, the natural and made materials make a good display.

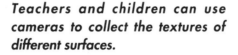

● Use soft pencils.
● A4 paper and a clip board or a sketchbook.
● Cameras.

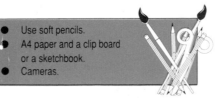

Printing textures with plasticene

- *Take a lump of old plasticene and flatten one side.*

- *Demonstrate how you can press the flat side of the plasticene on to a textured surface.*

- *Roll out some printing ink on to a plastic tray.*

- *Show the children how they can use the plasticene like a stamp.*

They will be making prints using imprints taken from the surfaces of different materials.

"What other textures could we find and print in this way? A good place to look is the playground. See what you can find. Choose one texture very carefully. Press the flat side of your plasticene into the texture and bring it back to the classroom.

Now you can make a print.

Start at the top and work down to cover all of the paper with the texture prints. Don't leave any big gaps. "

Why not pin the prints up immediately, in a block, to make a display of work in progress and to let the prints dry? It will then be easy to talk about the printed textures.

You can wash nearly all the ink off the plasticene which can then be re-used for more printing.

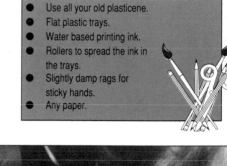

- Use all your old plasticene.
- Flat plastic trays.
- Water based printing ink.
- Rollers to spread the ink in the trays.
- Slightly damp rags for sticky hands.
- Any paper.

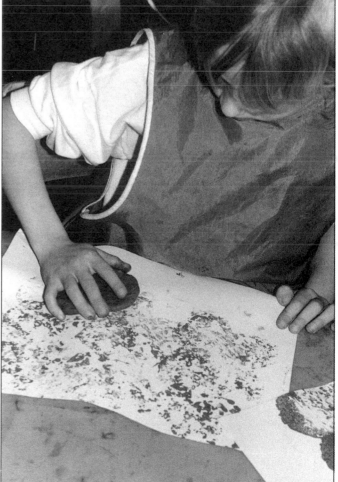

• • • • • Session 3 • • • • •

Exploring textures in clay

- *You will need to make some clay slabs.*

- *Place the clay on a board between two lengths of wood that have the same thickness.*

- *Roll the clay flat with a rolling pin. You will have a smooth slab of even thickness.*

- *Can the children make their own?*

- *Cut them into small squares or rectangles; 10cm square should be more than enough.*

- *If you make the slabs in advance cover them with cling film to keep them moist.*

"How could you make a texture in this clay slab? What could you use? Your finger? A clay tool? A lollypop stick? Has anyone got another idea?

Could somebody show us how to make a texture that looks really rough? Could somebody else make a texture that looks bumpy?

Could you each experiment and make a texture in your own clay slab?"

The children could draw a line in the middle of the clay slab so that they have two areas in which to make their textures.

Get the children to talk about their clay slabs. Compare the slabs to the textured materials they have collected.

- You will need all the equipment for using clay. See page 51.

Animals in clay

- *Make some more clay slabs.*

- *Before starting to work with the clay ask the children to look through books to find simple animal shapes. They can collect these shapes by drawing. They will need to have done work on shape first. See pages 15 and 16.*

- *Ask the children to imagine they could touch the animals. Talk about the textures of animal skins, coats and scales.*

"Here is a new clay slab. Draw the shape of your animal into the clay. Make your shape as large as you can.

You can cut the shape of an animal out of this slab. Has anyone had ideas about how you could cut the clay? You might need some practice!

When you have your animal shape cut out of the clay you can start to add texture."

It is difficult for Reception and Year 1 children to cut the clay shape out of the slab. Although many manage well, some may need help. Leave the animal shape flat on the board whilst they add the textures. You could go on to make ceramic tiles.

The children can work individually. A group of children can work together on a large slab of clay.

Drawing objects one at a time focusing on textures

You will need a number of objects with interesting and different textures, for example a cauliflower head, a ball of moss, a large spikey shell, a pineapple, a coconut, a soft toy...

This project will work best if the children have an awareness of shape. Look at page 15 and 16 for ideas about how to help children draw shapes.

The children will be drawing each object in turn to help them focus on textures.

● Ask the children to draw the shape of the first object they have chosen.

● Ask them to fill in the textures they can see with marks.

● Encourage them to go slowly and see how close their marks are to the textures of the object.

● When they have finished they can choose another object. An alternative approach is to start in the middle of the object and work towards the outside, building up the drawing with marks. They can add in outlines when they come to them.

" Feel your object carefully. Put it down and look at it. Can you see the way it feels?

How do you know something is rough without touching it with your hands?

Look at each little crevice, bump, furry or soft bit. This is like 'touching with your eyes'. "

Try making these texture drawings on large pieces of paper. You can use up to A1 size if you have the space. Young children will make large drawings if you ask them to think big. Marker pens are great for very large drawings. Ask the children to cover all the objects they have drawn with texture marks.

● Paper, small or large.
● Try charcoal, soft pencils, black wax crayons, marker pens.
● Drawing boards will be useful for large work.

76 TEXTURE

• • • • • Session 6 • • • • •

Talking about textures in paintings, drawings and sculptures

" We have been exploring textures. What about the different textures in this sculpture? How has this artist made different textures?

Can you say what the marks are like? Who can point out texture in the sculpture? To help we can look at our list of words or I can remind you of what we talked about when we were looking at textures.

Have you made any marks in your own drawings that look like the marks the artist made? "

You can often see how artists have painted, drawn or made textures. Talk about good examples with the children and ask them to make comparisons with textures in their own work.

Drawing a group of objects

This session should help children make still life drawings that have texture as a focus. Make a collection of natural objects that have different and interesting textures. This activity follows on naturally from session 5.

● *Talk about textures in the collection of natural objects.*

● *Ask the children to experiment with ways of making marks for the textures of the objects. See page 70 and 71.*

● *Draw the still life.*

Children will complain about 'making mistakes'. Convince them to keep going. A mistake made at the beginning of a drawing often seems much less important by the end.

● Paper, small or large.
● Try charcoal, soft pencils, black wax crayons, marker pens.
● Drawing boards will be useful for large work.

TEXTURE 77

LINE & MARK

• •

• • • • • • **Session 1** • • • • • •

Talking about line

Start off by showing the children how easy it is to draw a line.

❝I can make a line with a curve. What lines can you make? Who can make a new kind of line on the paper?

Try and think of a different way to make a line. ❞

Talk about all the possibilities with children. They will make lines that are wavy, zig-zag, straight, curling etc.

● *You will need an easel. Use a marker pen and at least one large sheet of paper.*

Experimenting by making lines

The children are now going to make their own lines.

❝Let's experiment. You are all going to make lots of different lines. I will call out a few to start with. Make a long bumpy line. Make a short spikey line...

Now experiment and make some lines of your own. You can put your lines anywhere on the paper. ❞

● Use pencils, markers, biros, notewriters, black wax crayons.
● Inexpensive paper is fine, use sheets that are as big as is practical.
● The drawing boards will help to create more space in the classroom if you want the whole class to work at the same time.

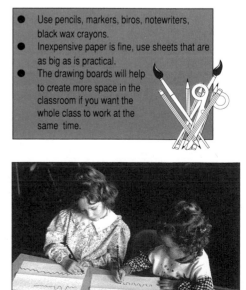

Lines and movement

- *Ideally you should do this in the playground or the hall.*

- *Ask the children to think up different ways of moving from one point in the hall to another.*

- *Children will run, hop, somersault, roll on their sides, shuffle, walk in slow motion, skip, leapfrog. They will have lots of ideas of their own.*

- *Give the children some paper and ask them to think up lines that to go with the movements.*

Talking about lines

There are lots of different ways of talking about these experiments. You could hold up one child's paper or ask the children to compare two experiments. Alternatively the children can identify particular lines and talk about what they are like.

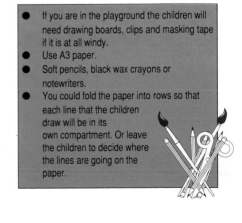

- If you are in the playground the children will need drawing boards, clips and masking tape if it is at all windy.
- Use A3 paper.
- Soft pencils, black wax crayons or notewriters.
- You could fold the paper into rows so that each line that the children draw will be in its own compartment. Or leave the children to decide where the lines are going on the paper.

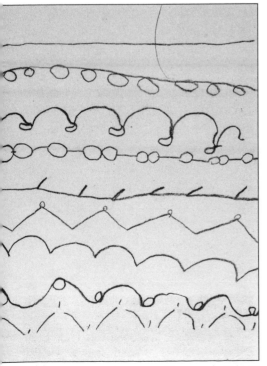

Choreography (Year 2)

Taking a line for a walk

This is an project that helps the children talk about a sequence of events.

"You are taking an invisible friend for a walk. Only you can see him or her. Your friend is very lively and never goes anywhere just by walking. He skips and jumps and hops and zig-zags and ... Tell me some of the other ways he can move.

Here is a large piece of paper and some wax crayons to draw with. Start anywhere you like on the paper and make a line to show what your friend does on the walk. Remember we can't see him, only the line he makes. You can go any where on the paper.

Why not draw in some of the things you and your invisible friend might see on the way? "

Using the line drawings as a prompt, ask individual children to tell the class what their invisible friend is doing and what they passed on the walk.

- Use a large sheet of paper and wax crayons.
- Have the children found out how to press harder with the wax crayons if they want to make stronger colours?

Looking for and drawing lines you can see

Go outside and ask the children to talk about all the different lines that they can see.

Use the discussion to focus the children before they draw. For example, they could draw trees in winter, the lines they can see on a building or wall, the horizon line etc.

As an alternative set up a washing line in the classroom.

The children could use notewriters, black biros, black wax crayons. These media will make good clear lines. Also the children can't rub them out. They have to keep going without worrying about mistakes. This may be difficult for them at first but it really does build confidence.

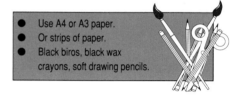
- Use A4 or A3 paper.
- Or strips of paper.
- Black biros, black wax crayons, soft drawing pencils.

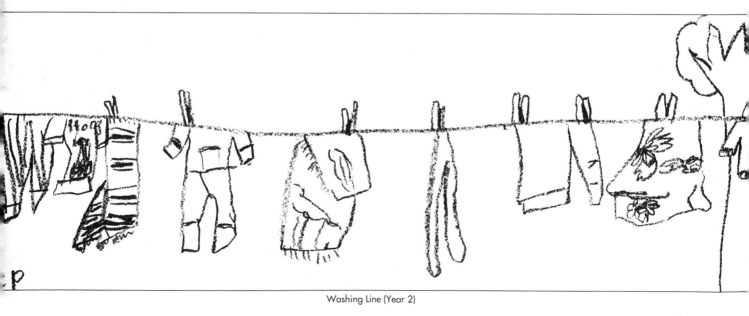

Washing Line (Year 2)

Experimenting with marks

- *Look at the projects on texture. For example see page 70. Here are some other ideas.*

- *Collect together different examples of all the drawing materials in the classroom that could be used to make marks.*

- *Fold large sheets of paper in half to divide them into two. On one side of the large sheet of paper ask the children to make one mark with each of the materials.*

- *Ask them to repeat this again on the second half of the paper but this time they must make sure that the new marks are really different from the first set.*

- *Ask the children how they made the marks look different.*

- *You could extend this project by exploring how some natural and made materials will make marks on paper. The children could also use paint and ink.*

Experimenting with marks and movement

This is great fun and very energetic!

- *You could use a roll of paper, long enough so that there is room for all the children to each have a space to draw.*

- *Split the class in half. Stand one half on each side of the paper.*

- *They will need something to make a marks with. Black wax crayons are fine.*

“How does a worm move? Let's all move like a worm. Now make a mark on the paper in front of you. Think about the wriggling worm.

How does a bee move? Let's all move like a bee. Now make your marks.

How does grass move in the wind? Let's all move like grass blowing gently in the wind. Now make a mark like the grass moving in the wind.

Now what ideas do you have?”

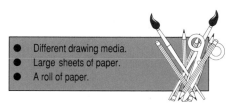

- Different drawing media.
- Large sheets of paper.
- A roll of paper.

• • • • • Session 4 • • • • •

Experimenting with marks and sounds

You will need a variety of musical instruments and other objects that the children could use to make sounds. They can also use their own voices.

Let the children decide where each mark is going on the paper. You could rule or fold the paper into rows or compartments, but you will need quite a few of these if you want the children to draw one line or mark in each space.

In this session the children have to make a conceptual leap between musical sounds and marks. Ask them to draw the sound not the instrument.

❝Listen to this sound. What is it like? A long rattle. Can you make a mark that goes with that sound?

Here is a cymbal crash. Can you make a mark to go with the crash?

Listen carefully. Listen to this sound. A loud sound, and then a soft sound, and then a loud sound on the recorder. Try a mark or line for that sound.

Now one of you come and make a sound for the others to try. Which instrument or object are you going to choose?

You can also make sounds with your voices. High, low, rattling, loud, very, very soft. Listen to each sound and make some marks or lines for these sounds too.❞

- You will need some large sheets of paper.
- Drawing materials that make strong, clear marks.
- Can the children choose from a variety of drawing media ?

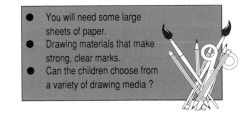

Talking about line and mark in a drawing or painting

Find a drawing or painting with a balanced variety of lines and marks. Perhaps you could look at ceramic decoration or fabric designs...

" Let's talk about what we can see.

Now let's talk about the different kinds of lines and marks. How do you think the artist made these lines? Could somebody demonstrate?

Let's all make lines in the air just like the artist made lines on the paper.

Now you could make your own lines and marks by drawing. "

It might help to use a view finder. This is a piece of card with a rectangle cut out. This acts as a frame to isolate part of the drawing or painting so that the children can concentrate on the lines and marks rather than on the picture.

In the photographs, the children went on to make imaginary sea drawings after exploring the line and marks they could see in a large pastel drawing of the sea, by the German artist Reiner Negrelli. This took place on a visit to the Glynn Vivian Art Gallery in Swansea.

Making a sea drawing focusing on line and mark

" I will read you something about the sea. Who has seen the sea? What is it like? How does the sea move? Who can make the movement of a wave? How would you move like a big wave?

How would you move like a calm, gentle sea? How would you move like the surf...the ripples...the splashes? What marks would go with those movements? Can you make the sounds too?

Remember the painting we looked at. Remember the marks you made with paint brushes. The artist used lots of different lines and marks and so did you. Remember how you made the movement of waves.

Build up your picture with marks. Fill up all the paper. "

Ask the children to talk about their work.

The initial discussion will help the children decide what kind of sea they are going to paint or draw. They could go on to put other things to do with the sea in their picture.

- You will need some large sheets of paper.
- Use pastels or charcoal and chalk. See page 37

LINE & MARK 83

APPENDIX

EQUIPMENT & MATERIALS
This list should provide a basis for ordering the materials and equipment needed for the projects described in the text. Although almost everything listed is mentioned in the book, neither the text nor the list can claim to be comprehensive.

Drawing
A2, A3, A4, A5, A6, white paper, use cartridge paper as funds allow. You will use far more of the A3 and A4 than other sizes
Newsprint or lining paper in sheets and from the roll
Buff, off white and grey sugar paper
Coloured sugar paper, including black
Thin white card
Drawing pencils, 4B are best
Black notewriters or any thin felt pens
Black wax crayons
Thick and thin black biros
Marker pens
Charcoal
Chalk
Coloured wax crayons
Coloured pencils and felt pens
Soft pastels
Inexpensive hairspray or fixative for charcoal and pastel drawings
Sketchbooks (not essential at Key Stage 1 but I recommend sketchbooks for Year 2 at least. Make up your own from A4 card, photocopy paper and black plastic binders)
A4 clipboards
Drawing boards
Bulldog clips
Masking tape
Easel for large group drawings and demonstrations

Collage
Scissors
Boards with a line drawn down the middle
PVA glue (Marvin Medium)
Small pots for glue
Glue spreaders
Newspapers and old magazines
Paper see 'drawing'
Rags

Printing
Old plasticene
Water based printing inks
Plastic trays
Rollers
Polystyrene tiles (Pressprint from Beryl)
Polystyrene meat trays
Paper see 'drawing'
Rags

Using clay
Clay, use buff colour clay if you want to paint the objects
Earthenware clay is rich red in colour. It is advisable not to mix different kinds of clay
Clay boards
Clay tools, (or use lollypop sticks, old cutlery etc.)
Sponges
Trays for the sponges
Small pots for slip
Brushes to apply slip
Rags
Shoe boxes or similar for storage

Painting
Readymix or powder paint, (see page 40 for advice about the range of colours to use)
Pots for the powder colour or six-well palettes for readymix paint
A flat mixing palette, use large tops to plastic food containers
Containers for water
Brushes, thick and thin
Paper, see 'drawing'
Rags

Fabric design and working with fabrics and thread
White material
Fabric crayons
An iron
Staple gun
Paper and drawing media for designing, see 'drawing'
Wood boards for streching the fabric
Assorted threads
Fabrics
Loom, see photograph on page 49 for a simple loom for Key Stage 1

Construction
Scrap cardboard
Wire (soft and pliable)
Wire cutters
Scrap wood
Assorted tools and materials for cutting and fixing

Computer aided design
Computer art software

Recording children's work
Clear plastic portfolio wallets to store children's work

EXAMPLES OF ART, CRAFT AND DESIGN VISIBLE IN THE PHOTOGRAPHS
Beckmann, Max
Self portrait p65

Burton, Andrew
Sculptures from a touring exhibition at the Glynn Vivian Art Gallery, Swansea, February 1993, p53, 57, 77

Ceramic domestic ware *p55*

Cezanne, Paul
Field at Jus de Bouffan p45

Fabrics *p32-33*

Jones, Christine
Coil Pot, 1987 p55

Kirchner, Ernst Ludwig
Hockey Players p19

Lindner, Richard
Cyclist p19

Matisse, Henri
The Purple Robe p38
Interior with Eggplants p27

Negrelli, Reiner
Wave, 1987, Permanent Collection, Glynn Vivian Art Gallery, Swansea p83

School Building *p22*

Wrapping papers *p31*

INDEX

GENERAL INDEX

TITLE	PRICE
NSEAD PUBLICATIONS	
TEACHING ART AT KEY STAGE 2 Nigel Meager	**£16.95**
A YEAR IN THE ART OF A PRIMARY SCHOOL Robert Clement and Liz Tarr	**£16.15**
ART MACHINE Edited by Arthur Hughes, Nick Stanley and John Swift	**£5.00**
DEPICTIONS OF AN ODYSSEY Peter MacKarrell, edited by Sheila Paine	**£11.40**
WHAT COLOUR IS THE WIND? Sue Blagden and John Everett	**£5.30**
GUIDE TO COURSES AND CAREERS IN ART, CRAFT AND DESIGN Tony Charlton	**£12.15**
NATIONAL CURRICULUM FOR ART – CURRENT ISSUES FOR CONSIDERATION Norman Binch and John Steers	**£2.95**
THE KEY STAGE 4 MAZE Michael Buchanan and Tim Royle	**£1.50**
DESIGNS WE LIVE BY Helga Loeb, Phil Slight and Nick Stanley	**£10.95**
NSEAD/LONGMAN PUBLICATIONS	
CRITICAL STUDIES IN ART AND DESIGN EDUCATION Edited by David Thistlewood	**£16.25**
DRAWING RESEARCH AND DEVELOPMENT Edited by David Thistlewood	**£15.70**
HISTORIES OF ART AND DESIGN EDUCATION Edited by David Thistlewood	**£15.20**

ALL PRICES INCLUDE POSTAGE & PACKING

NSEAD, The Gatehouse, Corsham Court, Corsham, Wiltshire SN13 0BZ
Tel: 01249 714825 Fax: 01249 716138

Printed by Pensord Press Ltd, Tram Road, Pontllanfraith, Blackwood, Gwent NP2 2YA